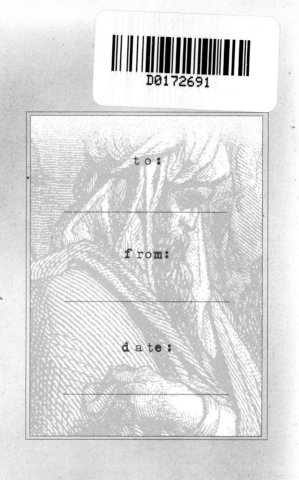

to:

_____

from:

_____

date:

_____

Promises
for a
Jesus Freak

dcTalk

BETHANY HOUSE
Minneapolis, Minnesota

Published by Bethany House Publishers
11400 Hampshire Avenue South
Bloomington, Minnesota 55438

Bethany House Publishers is a division of
Baker Publishing Group, Grand Rapids, Michigan.

Printed in the United States of America

ISBN   978-1-57778-210-0

TaBle of ConTeNts

Promises

I Want to Grow in God—
When You Desire Spiritual Maturity . . 96

Who Am I?—
Knowing Who You Are in Christ

Introduction

> By your words I can see where I'm going;
> they throw a beam of light on my dark path.
>
> PSALM 119:105 THE MESSAGE

God has given us His Word as a manual for life.
Everything we need, we can find in the Bible.
Direction, Hope, Wisdom, Instruction…God gives
us all these things through His Word.

Throughout history, Jesus Freaks have placed
great value upon God's Word. Many of them never
owned a Bible but cherished single Bible pages or
handwritten scriptures. Those who did own a Bible
were often persecuted or killed simply because
they were caught with a Bible.

In the 1970s, Communist soldiers in Asia
discovered an illegal Bible study. They told the
small congregation they would be let go as long as
they spit on "this book of lies." Some did. But one
young girl, overcome with love for her Savior,
knelt down and picked up the Bible. Using her
dress to wipe away the spit, she prayed, "Please

forgive them." A soldier put his pistol to her head and pulled the trigger.

The purpose of *Promises for a Jesus Freak* is to get you into God's Word. Use the scriptures here as a starting point. Find the verse or verses within a category that speaks the most to you. Then look it up in your Bible and read the entire chapter or story it came from. You will get the most out of each scripture if you read it in its context. Don't stop here. Go deeper. Like Job, you will say, "I have not departed from his commands but have treasured his words in my heart" (Job 23:12).

Help!—

When You Have a Need

Comfort—
When the World Seems Cold

"I will ask the Father to send you the Holy
Spirit who will help you and always be with
you. The Spirit will show you what is true.
The people of this world cannot accept the
Spirit, because they don't see or know him.
But you know the Spirit, who is with you
and will keep on living in you. I won't leave
you like orphans. I will come back to you."

JOHN 14:16-18 CEV

Even when the way goes through Death
Valley, I'm not afraid when you walk at my
side. Your trusty shepherd's crook makes me
feel secure.

PSALM 23:4 THE MESSAGE

You've kept track of my every toss and
turn through the sleepless nights, each tear
entered in your ledger, each ache written in
your book.

PSALM 56:8 THE MESSAGE

Comfort—
When the World Seems Cold

Remember your word to your servant, for you have given me hope. My comfort in my suffering is this: Your promise preserves my life. The arrogant mock me without restraint, but I do not turn from your law. I remember your ancient laws, O Lord, and I find comfort in them.

PSALM 119:49-52 NIV

Thank God, the Father of our Lord Jesus Christ, that he is our Father and the source of all mercy and comfort. For he gives us comfort in all our trials so that we in turn may be able to give the same sort of strong sympathy to others in theirs.

2 CORINTHIANS 1:3-4 PHILLIPS

The Lord is good. He protects those who trust him in times of trouble.

NAHUM 1:7 CEV

Comfort—
When the World Seems Cold

"I'm telling you these things while I'm still living with you. The Friend, the Holy Spirit whom the Father will send at my request, will make everything plain to you. He will remind you of all the things I have told you. I'm leaving you well and whole. That's my parting gift to you. Peace. I don't leave you the way you're used to being left—feeling abandoned, bereft. So don't be upset. Don't be distraught."

JOHN 14:26-27 THE MESSAGE

The Lord is a shelter for the oppressed, a refuge in times of trouble.

PSALM 9:9

Pile your troubles on GOD's shoulders— he'll carry your load, he'll help you out. He'll never let good people topple into ruin.

PSALM 55:22 THE MESSAGE

Confusion—
When I Don't Know What to Do

You give peace of mind to all who love your Law. Nothing can make them fall.

PSALM 119:165 CEV

Trust GOD from the bottom of your heart; don't try to figure out everything on your own. Listen for GOD's voice in everything you do, everywhere you go; he's the one who will keep you on track. Don't assume that you know it all.

PROVERBS 3:5-7 THE MESSAGE

"You will know the truth, and the truth will set you free."

JOHN 8:32 NIV

Confusion—
When I Don't Know What to Do

We often suffer, but we are never crushed. Even when we don't know what to do, we never give up. In times of trouble, God is with us, and when we are knocked down, we get up again.

2 CORINTHIANS 4:8-9 CEV

For God has not given us a spirit of cowardice, but a spirit of power and love and a sound mind.

2 TIMOTHY 1:7 PHILLIPS

"Who can know what the Lord is thinking? Who can give him counsel?" But we can understand these things, for we have the mind of Christ.

1 CORINTHIANS 2:16

Confusion—
When I Don't Know What to Do

Show me how you work, GOD; school me in your ways. Take me by the hand; lead me down the path of truth. You are my Savior, aren't you?

PSALM 25:5-6 THE MESSAGE

You will keep in perfect peace him whose mind is steadfast, because he trusts in you.

ISAIAH 26:3 NIV

I will listen to you, Lord God, because you promise peace to those who are faithful and no longer foolish.

PSALM 85:8 CEV

Courage—
When I Need to Be Bold

I eagerly expect and hope that I will in no way be ashamed, but will have sufficient courage so that now as always Christ will be exalted in my body, whether by life or by death. For to me, to live is Christ and to die is gain.

PHILIPPIANS 1:20-21 NIV

"Be strong and courageous! Do not be afraid of them! The Lord your God will go ahead of you. He will neither fail you nor forsake you."

DEUTERONOMY 31:6

I've commanded you to be strong and brave. Don't ever be afraid or discouraged! I am the Lord your God, and I will be there to help you wherever you go.

JOSHUA 1:9 CEV

Courage—
When I Need to Be Bold

If the old covenant, which has been set aside, was full of glory, then the new covenant, which remains forever, has far greater glory. Since this new covenant gives us such confidence, we can be very bold.

2 CORINTHIANS 3:11-12

The wicked are edgy with guilt, ready to run off even when no one's after them; honest people are relaxed and confident, bold as lions.

PROVERBS 28:1 THE MESSAGE

With all my heart I praise you, Lord. In the presence of angels I sing your praises. I worship at your holy temple and praise you for your love and your faithfulness. You were true to your word and made yourself more famous than ever before. When I asked for your help, you answered my prayer and gave me courage.

PSALM 138:1-3 CEV

Courage—
When I Need to Be Bold

For who is God except the Lord? Who but our God is a solid rock? God arms me with strength; he has made my way safe.

PSALM 18:31-32

The Lord is my strength and my shield; my heart trusts in him, and I am helped. My heart leaps for joy and I will give thanks to him in song.

PSALM 28:7 NIV

God is our refuge and strength, always ready to help in times of trouble. So we will not fear, even if earthquakes come and the mountains crumble into the sea.

PSALM 46:1-2

I am ready for anything through the strength of the One who lives within me.

PHILIPPIANS 4:13 PHILLIPS

Deliverance—
When I Need a Way Out

I run for dear life to GOD, I'll never live to regret it. Do what you do so well: get me out of this mess and up on my feet. Put your ear to the ground and listen, give me space for salvation.

PSALM 71:1-2 THE MESSAGE

"Now a slave has no permanent place in the family, but a son belongs to it forever. So if the Son sets you free, you will be free indeed."

JOHN 8:35-36 NIV

I love you, O Lord, my strength. The Lord is my rock, my fortress and my deliverer; my God is my rock, in whom I take refuge. He is my shield and the horn of my salvation, my stronghold. I call to the Lord, who is worthy of praise, and I am saved from my enemies.

PSALM 18:1-3 NIV

Deliverance—
When I Need a Way Out

Watch this: God's eye is on those who
respect him, the ones who are looking for his
love. He's ready to come to their rescue in
bad times; in lean times he keeps body and
soul together.

PSALM 33:18-19 THE MESSAGE

The ropes of death surrounded me; the
floods of destruction swept over me. The
grave wrapped its ropes around me; death
itself stared me in the face. But in my distress
I cried out to the Lord; yes, I prayed to my
God for help. He heard me from his
sanctuary; my cry reached his ears.

PSALM 18:4-6

Therefore let everyone who is godly pray
to you while you may be found; surely when
the mighty waters rise, they will not reach
him. You are my hiding place; you will
protect me from trouble and surround me
with songs of deliverance.

PSALM 32:6-7 NIV

Deliverance—
When I Need a Way Out

I am the Lord your God, and I will rescue you from all your enemies.

2 KINGS 17:39 CEV

I think you ought to know, dear brothers and sisters, about the trouble we went through in the province of Asia. We were crushed and completely overwhelmed, and we thought we would never live through it. In fact, we expected to die. But as a result, we learned not to rely on ourselves, but on God who can raise the dead. And he did deliver us from mortal danger. And we are confident that he will continue to deliver us.

2 CORINTHIANS 1:8-10

"Because he loves me," says the LORD, "I will rescue him; I will protect him, for he acknowledges my name. He will call upon me, and I will answer him; I will be with him in trouble, I will deliver him and honor him. With long life will I satisfy him and show him my salvation."

PSALM 91:14-16 NIV

Defense—
When I Face an Enemy

"There is no one like the God of Jeshurun, who rides on the heavens to help you and on the clouds in his majesty. The eternal God is your refuge, and underneath are the everlasting arms. He will drive out your enemy before you, saying, 'Destroy him!'"

DEUTERONOMY 33:26-27 NIV

On the day disaster struck they came and attacked, but you defended me. When I was fenced in, you freed and rescued me because you love me.

2 SAMUEL 22:19-20 CEV

Oh, please help us against our enemies, for all human help is useless. With God's help we will do mighty things, for he will trample down our foes.

PSALM 60:11-12

Defense—
When I Face an Enemy

The Lord has taken away your
punishment, he has turned back your enemy.
The Lord, the King of Israel, is with you;
never again will you fear any harm…. The
Lord your God is with you, he is mighty to
save. He will take great delight in you, he
will quiet you with his love, he will rejoice
over you with singing.

ZEPHANIAH 3:15, 17 NIV

"I have given you authority over all the
power of the enemy, and you can walk
among snakes and scorpions and crush them.
Nothing will injure you."

LUKE 10:19

My help and glory are in God—granite-
strength and safe-harbor-God—So trust him
absolutely, people; lay your lives on the line
for him. God is a safe place to be.

PSALM 62:7-8 THE MESSAGE

Defense—
When I Face an Enemy

Stronger than wild sea storms, mightier than sea-storm breakers, Mighty GOD rules from High Heaven.

PSALM 93:4 THE MESSAGE

Our Lord is great and powerful! He understands everything. The Lord helps the poor, but he smears the wicked in the dirt.

PSALM 147:5-6 CEV

In conclusion be strong—not in yourselves but in the Lord, in the power of his boundless strength. Put on God's complete armour so that you can successfully resist all the devil's craftiness.

EPHESIANS 6:10-11 PHILLIPS

Depression—
When I Want to Feel Joy and Peace Again

Surely God does not reject a blameless man or strengthen the hands of evildoers. He will yet fill your mouth with laughter and your lips with shouts of joy.

JOB 8:20-21 NIV

I have God's more-than-enough, more joy in one ordinary day than they get in all their shopping sprees. At day's end I'm ready for sound sleep, for you, God have put my life back together.

PSALM 4:7-8 THE MESSAGE

I praise you, Lord for being my guide. Even in the darkest night, your teachings fill my mind. I will always look to you, as you stand beside me and protect me from fear.

PSALM 16:7-8 CEV

Depression—
When I Want to Feel Joy and Peace Again

You have turned my sorrow into joyful dancing. No longer am I sad and wearing sackcloth. I thank you from my heart, and I will never stop singing your praises, my Lord and my God.

PSALM 30:11-12 CEV

Give your servant a happy life; I put myself in your hands! You're well-known and good and forgiving, bighearted to all who ask for help.

PSALM 86:4 THE MESSAGE

May the God of hope fill you with all joy and peace in your faith, that by the power of the Holy Spirit, your whole life and outlook may be radiant with hope.

ROMANS 15:13 PHILLIPS

Depression—
When I Want to Feel Joy and Peace Again

"Though the mountains be shaken and the hills be removed, yet my unfailing love for you will not be shaken nor my covenant of peace be removed," says the LORD, who has compassion on you.

ISAIAH 54:10 NIV

If our minds are ruled by our desires, we will die. But if our minds are ruled by the Spirit, we will have life and peace.

ROMANS 8:6 CEV

Don't worry over anything whatever; whenever you pray tell God every detail of your needs in thankful prayer, and the peace of God, which surpasses human understanding, will keep constant guard over your hearts and minds as they rest in Christ Jesus.

PHILIPPIANS 4:6-7 PHILLIPS

Direction—
When I Don't Know Which Way to Go

GOD is fair and just; he corrects the misdirected, sends them in the right direction. He gives the rejects his hand, and leads them step by step. From now on every road you travel will take you to GOD. Follow the Covenant signs; read the charted directions.

PSALM 25:8-10 THE MESSAGE

"In your unfailing love you will lead the people you have redeemed. In your strength you will guide them to your holy dwelling."

EXODUS 15:13 NIV

Show me the path where I should walk, O Lord; point out the right road for me to follow. Lead me by your truth and teach me, for you are the God who saves me. All day long I put my hope in you.

PSALM 25:4-5

Direction—
When I Don't Know Which Way to Go

You, Lord God, are my mighty rock and my fortress. Lead me and guide me, so that your name will be honored.

PSALM 31:3 CEV

For that is what God is like. He is our God forever and ever, and he will be our guide until we die.

PSALM 48:14

Ask me, and I will tell you things that you don't know and can't find out.

JEREMIAH 33:3 CEV

Direction—
When I Don't Know Which Way to Go

"When the Spirit of truth comes, he will guide you into all truth. He will not be presenting his own ideas; he will be telling you what he has heard. He will tell you about the future."

JOHN 16:13

The LORD says, "I will guide you along the best pathway for your life. I will advise you and watch over you."

PSALM 32:8

I am always with you; you hold me by my right hand. You guide me with your counsel, and afterward you will take me into glory.

PSALM 73:23-24 NIV

Emotional Healing—
When My Heart Is Broken

The Lord doesn't hate or despise the helpless in all of their troubles. When I cried out, he listened and did not turn away.

PSALM 22:24 CEV

Heart-shattered lives ready for love don't for a moment escape God's notice.

PSALM 51:17 THE MESSAGE

From the ends of the earth I call to you, I call as my heart grows faint; lead me to the rock that is higher than I. For you have been my refuge, a strong tower against the foe.

PSALM 61:2-3 NIV

Emotional Healing—
When My Heart Is Broken

My health may fail, and my spirit may grow weak, but God remains the strength of my heart; he is mine forever.

PSALM 73:26

You can throw the whole weight of your anxieties upon him, for you are his personal concern.

1 PETER 5:7 PHILLIPS

But you, O Sovereign Lord, deal well with me for your name's sake; out of the goodness of your love, deliver me. For I am poor and needy, and my heart is wounded within me.

PSALM 109:21-22 NIV

Emotional Healing—
When My Heart Is Broken

Our holy God lives forever in the highest heavens, and this is what he says: Though I live high above in the holy place, I am here to help those who are humble and depend only on me.

ISAIAH 57:15 CEV

He heals the heartbroken and bandages their wounds.

PSALM 147:3 THE MESSAGE

The Lord is close to the brokenhearted; he rescues those who are crushed in spirit.

PSALM 34:18

"The Spirit of the Lord is upon me, because he anointed me to preach good tidings to the poor: He hath sent me to proclaim release to the captives, and recovering of sight to the blind, to set at liberty them that are bruised, to proclaim the acceptable year of the Lord."

LUKE 4:18 PHILLIPS

False Accusations—
When the Finger of Blame Is Pointing at Me

Have mercy on me, O God, have mercy! I look to you for protection. I will hide beneath the shadow of your wings until this violent storm is past. I cry out to God Most High, to God who will fulfill his purpose for me. He will send help from heaven to save me, rescuing me from those who are out to get me.

PSALM 57:1-3

"No weapon forged against you will prevail, and you will refute every tongue that accuses you. This is the heritage of the servants of the Lord, and this is their vindication from me," declares the Lord.

ISAIAH 54:17 NIV

When I walk into the thick of trouble, keep me alive in the angry turmoil. With one hand strike my foes, with your other hand save me.

PSALM 138:7 THE MESSAGE

False Accusations—
When the Finger of Blame Is Pointing at Me

"Blessed are you when people insult you, persecute you and falsely say all kinds of evil against you because of me."

MATTHEW 5:11 NIV

God, don't just watch from the sidelines. Come on! Run to my side! My accusers— make them lose face. Those out to get me— make them look like idiots, while I stretch out, reaching for you, and daily add praise to praise.

PSALM 71:12-14 THE MESSAGE

The Lord God keeps me from being disgraced. So I refuse to give up, because I know God will never let me down. My protector is nearby; no one can stand here to accuse me of wrong. The Lord God will help me and prove I am innocent. My accusers will wear out like moth-eaten clothes.

ISAIAH 50:7-9 CEV

False Accusations—
When the Finger of Blame Is Pointing at Me

Though everyone else in the world is a liar, God is true. As the Scriptures say, "He will be proved right in what he says, and he will win his case in court."

ROMANS 3:4

Be careful how you live among your unbelieving neighbors. Even if they accuse you of doing wrong, they will see your honorable behavior, and they will believe and give honor to God when he comes to judge the world.

1 PETER 2:12

Don't try to get even. Trust the Lord and he will help you.

PROVERBS 20:22 CEV

Truth will last forever; lies are soon found out.

PROVERBS 12:19 CEV

Favor—
When I Need to Be Seen through God's Eyes

Let all who take refuge in you be glad; let them ever sing for joy. Spread your protection over them, that those who love your name may rejoice in you. For surely, O LORD, you bless the righteous; you surround them with your favor as with a shield.

PSALM 5:11-12 NIV

A sterling reputation is better than striking it rich; a gracious spirit is better than money in the bank.

PROVERBS 22:1 THE MESSAGE

They did not conquer the land with their swords; it was not their own strength that gave them victory. It was by your mighty power that they succeeded; it was because you favored them and smiled on them.

PSALM 44:3

Favor—
When I Need to Be Seen through God's Eyes

Come to my home each day and listen to me [wisdom]. You will find happiness. By finding me, you find life, and the Lord will be pleased with you.

PROVERBS 8:34-35 CEV

Let love and faithfulness never leave you; bind them around your neck, write them on the tablet of your heart. Then you will win favor and a good name in the sight of God and man.

PROVERBS 3:3-4 NIV

Then the patriarchs in their jealousy of Joseph sold him as a slave into Egypt. But God was with him and saved him from all his troubles and gave him favour and wisdom in the eyes of Pharaoh the king of Egypt. Pharaoh made him governor of Egypt and put him in charge of his own entire household.

ACTS 7:9-10 PHILLIPS

Favor—
When I Need to Be Seen through God's Eyes

If you are pleased with me, teach me your ways so I may know you and continue to find favor with you. Remember that this nation is your people.

EXODUS 33:13 NIV

Sing to the Lord, all you godly ones! Praise his holy name. His anger lasts for a moment, but his favor lasts a lifetime! Weeping may go on all night, but joy comes with the morning.

PSALM 30:4-5

For the LORD God is a sun and shield; the LORD bestows favor and honor; no good thing does he withhold from those whose walk is blameless.

PSALM 84:11 NIV

Fear—
When I Feel Afraid

Do not be afraid or discouraged, for the Lord is the one who goes before you. He will be with you; he will neither fail you nor forsake you.

DEUTERONOMY 31:8

Light, space, zest—that's GOD! So, with him on my side I'm fearless, afraid of no one and nothing.

PSALM 27:1 THE MESSAGE

When I am afraid, I will trust in you. In God, whose word I praise, in God I trust; I will not be afraid. What can mortal man do to me?

PSALM 56:3-4 NIV

Fear—
When I Feel Afraid

"Peace I leave with you; my peace I give you. I do not give to you as the world gives. Do not let your hearts be troubled and do not be afraid."

JOHN 14:27 NIV

Even when I walk through the dark valley of death, I will not be afraid, for you are close beside me. Your rod and your staff protect and comfort me.

PSALM 23:4

I trust you to save me, Lord God, and I won't be afraid. My power and my strength come from you, and you have saved me.

ISAIAH 12:2 CEV

God is a safe place to hide, ready to help when we need him. We stand fearless at the cliff-edge of doom, courageous in seastorm and earthquake, before the rush and roar of oceans, the tremors that shift mountains.

PSALM 46:1-3 THE MESSAGE

Fear—
When I Feel Afraid

Don't be afraid of sudden disasters or storms that strike those who are evil. You can be sure that the Lord will protect you from harm.

PROVERBS 3:25-26 CEV

Do not be afraid of the terrors of the night, nor fear the dangers of the day, nor dread the plague that stalks in darkness, nor the disaster that strikes at midday. Though a thousand fall at your side, though ten thousand are dying around you, these evils will not touch you.

PSALM 91:5-7

Don't be afraid. I am with you. Don't tremble with fear. I am your God. I will make you strong, as I protect you with my arm and give you victories.

ISAIAH 41:10 CEV

Grief—
When I've Lost Someone I Love

Listen, and I will tell you a secret. We shall not all die, but suddenly, in the twinkling of an eye, every one of us will be changed as the trumpet sounds! For the trumpet will sound and the dead shall be raised beyond the reach of corruption, and we shall be changed. For this perishable nature of ours must be wrapped in imperishability, these bodies which are mortal must be wrapped in immortality. So when the perishable is lost in the imperishable, the mortal lost in the immortal, this scripture will come true: Death is swallowed up in victory. Where now O death, is your victory; where now is your stinging power? It is sin which gives death its sting, and it is the Law which gives sin its power. All thanks to God, then, who gives us the victory over these things through our Lord Jesus Christ!

1 CORINTHIANS 15:51-57 PHILLIPS

Even though I walk through the valley of the shadow of death, I will fear no evil, for you are with me; your rod and your staff, they comfort me.

PSALM 23:4 NIV

Grief—
When I've Lost Someone I Love

The Lord All-Powerful will destroy the power of death and wipe away all tears. No longer will his people be insulted everywhere. The Lord has spoken!

ISAIAH 25:8 CEV

"How happy are those who know what sorrow means, for they will be given courage and comfort!"

MATTHEW 5:4 PHILLIPS

"It's urgent that you get this right: The time has arrived—I mean right now!—when dead men and women will hear the voice of the Son of God and, hearing, will come alive. Just as the Father has life in himself, he has conferred on the Son life in himself."

JOHN 5:25 THE MESSAGE

"And this is the will of the One who sent me, that everyone who sees the Son and trusts him should have eternal life, and I will raise him up when the last day comes."

JOHN 6:40 PHILLIPS

Grief—
When I've Lost Someone I Love

"Do not let your hearts be troubled. Trust in God; trust also in me."

JOHN 14:1 NIV

If we have hope in Christ only for this life, we are the most miserable people in the world. But the fact is that Christ has been raised from the dead. He has become the first of a great harvest of those who will be raised to life again.

1 CORINTHIANS 15:19-20

Everybody dies in Adam; everybody comes alive in Christ.

1 CORINTHIANS 15:22 THE MESSAGE

My friends, we want you to understand how it will be for those followers who have already died. Then you won't grieve over them and be like people who don't have any hope. We believe that Jesus died and was raised to life. We also believe that when God brings Jesus back again, he will bring with him all who had faith in Jesus before they died.

1 THESSALONIANS 4:13-15 CEV

Healing—
When I Need a Touch from God

Praise the Lord, O my soul, and forget not
all his benefits—who forgives all your sins
and heals all your diseases.

PSALM 103:2-3 NIV

He suffered and endured great pain for us,
but we thought his suffering was punishment
from God. He was wounded and crushed
because of our sins; by taking our
punishment, he made us completely well.

ISAIAH 53:4-5 CEV

Word got around the entire Roman
province of Syria. People brought anybody
with an ailment, whether mental, emotional,
or physical. Jesus healed them, one and all.

MATTHEW 4:23 THE MESSAGE

Healing—
When I Need a Touch from God

If anyone is ill he should send for the church elders. They should pray over him, anointing him with oil in the Lord's name. Believing prayer will save the sick man; the Lord will restore him and any sins that he has committed will be forgiven.

JAMES 5:14-15 PHILLIPS

Worship the Lord your God, and his blessing will be on your food and water. I will take away sickness from among you.

EXODUS 23:25 NIV

That evening many demon-possessed people were brought to Jesus. All the spirits fled when he commanded them to leave; and he healed all the sick. This fulfilled the word of the Lord through Isaiah, who said, "He took our sicknesses and removed our diseases."

MATTHEW 8:16-17

Healing—
When I Need a Touch from God

And he personally bore our sins in his own body on the cross, so that we might be dead to sin and be alive to all that is good. It was the suffering that he bore which has healed you.

1 PETER 2:24 PHILLIPS

He spoke the word that healed you, that pulled you back from the brink of death. So thank GOD for his marvelous love, for his miracle mercy to the children he loves.

PSALM 107:20-21 THE MESSAGE

My prayer for you, my very dear friend, is that you may be as healthy and prosperous in every way as you are in soul.

3 JOHN 2 PHILLIPS

Hope—
When I Feel Like Giving Up

It is true that he was destined for this purpose before the world was founded, but it was for your benefit that he was revealed in these last days—for you who found your faith in God through him. And God raised him from the dead and gave him heavenly splendour, so that all your faith and hope might be centered in God.

1 PETER 1:20-21 PHILLIPS

The eyes of the Lord are on those who fear him, on those whose hope is in his unfailing love, to deliver them from death and keep them alive in famine. We wait in hope for the Lord; he is our help and our shield. In him our hearts rejoice, for we trust in his holy name. May your unfailing love rest upon us, O Lord, even as we put our hope in you.

PSALM 33:18-22 NIV

Hope—
When I Feel Like Giving Up

Why are you down in the dumps, dear soul? Why are you crying the blues? Fix my eyes on God—soon I'll be praising again. He puts a smile on my face. He's my God.

PSALM 42:5-6 THE MESSAGE

Show me the path where I should walk, O Lord; point out the right road for me to follow. Lead me by your truth and teach me, for you are the God who saves me. All day long I put my hope in you.

PSALM 25:4-5

You are my place of safety and my shield. Your word is my only hope.

PSALM 119:114 CEV

I wait for the Lord, my soul waits, and in his word I put my hope.

PSALM 130:5 NIV

Wisdom is sweet to your soul. If you find it, you will have a bright future, and your hopes will not be cut short.

PROVERBS 24:14

Hope—
When I Feel Like Giving Up

I wait quietly before God, for my hope is in him. He alone is my rock and my salvation, my fortress where I will not be shaken.

PSALM 62:5-6

God our Father loves us. He is kind and has given us eternal comfort and a wonderful hope. We pray that our Lord Jesus Christ and God our Father will encourage you and help you always to do and say the right thing.

2 THESSALONIANS 2:16-17 CEV

May the God of hope fill you with all joy and peace in your faith, that by the power of the Holy Spirit, your whole life and outlook may be radiant with hope.

ROMANS 15:13 PHILLIPS

Imprisonment—
What If I Am Jailed for My Faith?

They put cruel chains on his ankles, an iron collar around his neck, until God's word came to the Pharaoh, and GOD confirmed his promise. God sent the king to release him. The Pharaoh set Joseph free; he appointed him master of his palace, put him in charge of all his business to personally instruct his princes and train his advisors in wisdom.

PSALM 105:18-21 THE MESSAGE

I cried out to the Lord, and he answered me from his holy mountain. I lay down and slept. I woke up in safety, for the Lord was watching over me. I am not afraid of ten thousand enemies who surround me on every side.

PSALM 3:4-6

Though an army besiege me, my heart will not fear; though war break out against me, even then will I be confident. One thing I ask of the Lord, this is what I seek: that I may dwell in the house of the Lord all the days of my life, to gaze upon the beauty of the Lord and to seek him in his temple. For in the day of trouble he will keep me safe in his dwelling; he will hide me in the shelter of his tabernacle and set me high upon a rock.

PSALM 27:3-5 NIV

Imprisonment—
What If I Am Jailed for My Faith?

Then, after giving them a severe beating, they threw them into prison, instructing the jailer to keep them safe. On receiving such strict orders, he hustled them into the inner jail and fastened their feet securely in the stocks. But about midnight Paul and Silas were praying and singing hymns to God while the other prisoners were listening to them. Suddenly there was a great earthquake, big enough to shake the foundations of the prison. Immediately all the doors flew open and everyone's chains were unfastened.

ACTS 16:23-26 PHILLIPS

Do you think anyone is going to be able to drive a wedge between us and Christ's love for us? There is no way! Not trouble, not hard times, not hatred, not hunger, not homelessness, not bullying threats, not backstabbing, not even the worst sins listed in Scripture…. None of this fazes us because Jesus loves us. I'm absolutely convinced that nothing—nothing living or dead, angelic or demonic, today or tomorrow, high or low, thinkable or unthinkable—absolutely *nothing* can get between us and God's love because of the way that Jesus our Master has embraced us.

ROMANS 8:35-37 THE MESSAGE

Imprisonment—
What If I Am Jailed for My Faith?

We expected to die. But as a result, we
learned not to rely on ourselves, but on God
who can raise the dead. And he did deliver
us from mortal danger. And we are confident
that he will continue to deliver us.

2 CORINTHIANS 1:9-10

This is the reason why we never lose
heart. The outward man does indeed suffer
wear and tear, but every day the inward man
receives fresh strength. These little troubles
(which are really so transitory) are winning
for us a permanent, glorious and solid reward
out of all proportion to our pain.

2 CORINTHIANS 4:16-17 PHILLIPS

But he replied, "My kindness is all you
need. My power is strongest when you are
weak." So if Christ keeps giving me his power,
I will gladly brag about how weak I am. Yes, I
am glad to be weak or insulted or mistreated
or to have troubles and sufferings, if it is for
Christ. Because when I am weak, I am strong.

2 CORINTHIANS 12:9-10 CEV

Therefore I, a prisoner for serving the
Lord, beg you to lead a life worthy of your
calling, for you have been called by God.

EPHESIANS 4:1

Injustice—
When It Just Doesn't Seem Fair

"God will bless you when people insult you, mistreat you, and tell all kinds of evil lies about you because of me."

MATTHEW 5:11 CEV

God's a safe-house for the battered, a sanctuary during bad times. The moment you arrive, you relax; you're never sorry you knocked.

PSALM 9:10 THE MESSAGE

Another of his disciples said, "Lord, first let me return home and bury my father." But Jesus told him, "Follow me now! Let those who are spiritually dead care for their own dead."

MATTHEW 8:21-22

We, therefore, can confidently say: The Lord is my helper; I will not fear: What shall man do unto me?

HEBREWS 13:6 PHILLIPS

Injustice—
When It Just Doesn't Seem Fair

"When you stand praying, if you hold anything against anyone, forgive him, so that your Father in heaven may forgive you your sins."

MARK 11:25 NIV

Let there be no more bitter resentment or anger, no more shouting or slander, and let there be no bad feeling of any kind among you. Be kind to each other, be compassionate. Be as ready to forgive others as God for Christ's sake has forgiven you.

EPHESIANS 4:31-32 PHILLIPS

Don't let evil get the best of you, but conquer evil by doing good.

ROMANS 12:21

Injustice—
When It Just Doesn't Seem Fair

Anyone who does wrong will be repaid for his wrong, and there is no favoritism.

COLOSSIANS 3:25 NIV

He was quite explicit: "Vengeance is mine, and I won't overlook a thing," and, "God will judge his people." Nobody's getting by with anything, believe me.

HEBREWS 10:30 THE MESSAGE

In face of all this, what is there left to say? If God is for us, who can be against us? He who did not grudge his own Son but gave him up for us all—can we not trust such a God to give us, with him, everything else that we can need?

ROMANS 8:31-32 PHILLIPS

Jealousy—
When I Just Can't See Past It

Don't envy bad people; don't even want to be around them. All they think about is causing a disturbance; all they talk about is making trouble.

PROVERBS 24:1 THE MESSAGE

Don't be jealous of cruel people or follow their example.

PROVERBS 3:31 CEV

We should be decent and true in everything we do, so that everyone can approve of our behavior. Don't participate in wild parties and getting drunk, or in adultery and immoral living, or in fighting and jealousy. But let the Lord Jesus Christ take control of you, and don't think of ways to indulge your evil desires.

ROMANS 13:13-14

Jealousy—
When I Just Can't See Past It

A heart at peace gives life to the body, but envy rots the bones.

PROVERBS 14:30 NIV

For you are still unspiritual; all the time that there is jealousy and squabbling among you you show that you are—you are living just like men of the world.

1 CORINTHIANS 3:3 PHILLIPS

Love is kind and patient, never jealous, boastful, proud, or rude. Love isn't selfish or quick tempered. It doesn't keep a record of wrongs that others do.

1 CORINTHIANS 13:4 CEV

Those who belong to Christ Jesus have crucified their lower nature with all that it loved and lusted for. If our lives are centred in the Spirit, let us be guided by the Spirit. Let us not be ambitious for our own reputations, for that only means making each other jealous.

GALATIANS 5:24-26 PHILLIPS

Jealousy—
When I Just Can't See Past It

So get rid of all malicious behavior and deceit. Don't just pretend to be good! Be done with hypocrisy and jealousy and backstabbing. You must crave pure spiritual milk so that you can grow into the fullness of your salvation. Cry out for this nourishment as a baby cries for milk.

1 PETER 2:1-2

Is there some wise and understanding man among you? Then let his life be a shining example of the humility that is born of true wisdom. But if your heart is full of bitter jealousy and rivalry, then do not boast and do not deny the truth. You may acquire a certain wisdom, but it does not come from above—it comes from this world, from your own lower nature, even from the devil. For wherever you find jealousy and rivalry you also find disharmony and all other kinds of evil.

JAMES 3:13-16 PHILLIPS

Joy—
When I Need a Real Thrill

I'm happy from the inside out, and from the outside in, I'm firmly formed. You canceled my ticket to hell—that's not my destination!

PSALM 16:9-10 THE MESSAGE

The commandments of the Lord are right, bringing joy to the heart. The commands of the Lord are clear, giving insight to life.

PSALM 19:8

The Lord is my strength and my shield; my heart trusts in him, and I am helped. My heart leaps for joy and I will give thanks to him in song.

PSALM 28:7 NIV

With joy you will drink deeply from the fountain of salvation!

ISAIAH 12:3

joy—
When I Need a Real Thrill

"If you keep my commandments you will live in my love just as I have kept my Father's commandments and live in his love. I have told you this so that you can share my joy, and that your joy may be complete."

JOHN 15:10-11 PHILLIPS

God's kingdom isn't about eating and drinking. It is about pleasing God, about living in peace, and about true happiness. All this comes from the Holy Spirit.

ROMANS 14:17 CEV

The Lord has done great things for us, and we are filled with joy.

PSALM 126:3 NIV

Joy—
When I Need a Real Thrill

The Spirit, however, produces in human
life fruits such as these: love, joy, peace,
patience, kindness, generosity, fidelity,
tolerance and self-control—and no law exists
against any of them.

GALATIANS 5:22 PHILLIPS

There is deceit in the hearts of those who
plot evil, but joy for those who promote peace.

PROVERBS 12:20 NIV

You love him even though you have never
seen him. At present you trust him without
being able to see him. Though you do not
see him, you trust him; and even now you
are happy with a glorious, inexpressible joy.
Your reward for trusting him will be the
salvation of your souls.

1 PETER 1:8-9

Loneliness—
When I Feel Like No One Understands Me

"Be sure of this: I am with you always, even to the end of the age."

MATTHEW 28:20

Is there anyplace I can go to avoid your Spirit? To be out of your sight? If I climb to the sky, you're there! If I go underground, you're there! If I flew on morning's wings to the far western horizon, you'd find me in a minute—you're already there waiting! Then I said to myself, "Oh, he even sees me in the dark! At night I'm immersed in the light!"

PSALM 139:7-10 THE MESSAGE

Who can separate us from the love of Christ? Can trouble, pain or persecution? Can lack of clothes and food, danger to life and limb, the threat of force of arms?

ROMANS 8:35 PHILLIPS

Loneliness—
When I Feel Like No One Understands Me

Keep your lives free from the lust for money: be content with what you have. God has said: I will in no wise fail thee, neither will I in any wise forsake thee.

HEBREWS 13:5 PHILLIPS

Our God, from your sacred home you take care of orphans and protect widows. You find families for those who are lonely. You set prisoners free and let them prosper, but all who rebel will live in a scorching desert.

PSALM 68:5-6 CEV

The eternal God is your refuge, and underneath are the everlasting arms. He will drive out your enemy before you, saying, "Destroy him!"

DEUTERONOMY 33:27 NIV

Loneliness—
When I Feel Like No One Understands Me

Those who know your name will trust in you, for you, Lord, have never forsaken those who seek you.

PSALM 9:10 NIV

I have become absolutely convinced that neither death nor life, neither messenger of Heaven nor monarch of earth, neither what happens today nor what may happen tomorrow, neither a power from on high nor a power from below, nor anything else in God's whole world has any power to separate us from the love of God in Jesus Christ our Lord!

ROMANS 8:38-39 PHILLIPS

How precious are your thoughts about me, O God! They are innumerable! I can't even count them; they outnumber the grains of sand! And when I wake up in the morning, you are still with me!

PSALM 139:17-18

Love—
When I Need to Know God Loves Me

To us, the greatest demonstration of God's love for us has been his sending his only Son into the world to give us life through him. We see real love, not in that fact that we loved God, but that he loved us and sent his Son to make personal atonement for our sins.

1 JOHN 4:9-10 PHILLIPS

You are merciful, Lord! You are kind and patient and always loving.

PSALM 145:8 CEV

I'm absolutely convinced that nothing—nothing living or dead, angelic or demonic, today or tomorrow, high or low, thinkable or unthinkable—absolutely *nothing* can get between us and God's love because of the way that Jesus our Master has embraced us.

ROMANS 8:38-39 THE MESSAGE

Love—
When I Need to Know God Loves Me

But when the kindness and love of God our Saviour dawned upon us, he saved us in his mercy—not by virtue of any moral achievements of ours, but by the cleansing power of a new birth and the renewal of the Holy Spirit, which he poured upon us through Jesus Christ our Saviour.

TITUS 3:4-7 PHILLIPS

But I trust in your unfailing love; my heart rejoices in your salvation. I will sing to the Lord, for he has been good to me.

PSALM 13:5-6 NIV

I will be glad and rejoice in your love, for you saw my affliction and knew the anguish of my soul. You have not handed me over to the enemy but have set my feet in a spacious place.

PSALM 31:7-8 NIV

Love—
When I Need to Know God Loves Me

God-defiers are always in trouble; God-affirmers find themselves loved every time they turn around.

PSALM 32:10 THE MESSAGE

Your love is faithful, Lord, and even the clouds in the sky can depend on you. Your decisions are always fair. They are firm like mountains, deep like the sea, and all people and animals are under your care. Your love is a treasure, and everyone finds shelter in the shadow of your wings.

PSALM 36:5-7 CEV

God is love. When we take up permanent residence in a life of love, we live in God and God lives in us. This way, love has the run of the house, becomes at home and mature in us, so that we're free of worry on Judgment Day—our standing in the world is identical with Christ's. There is no room in love for fear. Well-formed love banishes fear. Since fear is crippling, a fearful life—fear of death, fear of judgment—is one not yet fully formed in love.

1 JOHN 4:16-18 THE MESSAGE

Peace—
When I Need a Quiet Mind

May the Lord bless you and protect you.
May the Lord smile on you and be gracious
to you. May the Lord show you his favor and
give you his peace.

NUMBERS 6:24-26

"I give you peace, the kind of peace that
only I can give. It isn't like the peace that this
world can give. So don't be worried or afraid."

JOHN 14:27 CEV

You will keep in perfect peace him whose
mind is steadfast, because he trusts in you.
Trust in the Lord forever, for the Lord, the
Lord, is the Rock eternal.

ISAIAH 26:3-4 NIV

Peace—
When I Need a Quiet Mind

I listen carefully to what God the Lord is saying, for he speaks peace to his people, his faithful ones. But let them not return to their foolish ways.

PSALM 85:8

GOD makes his people strong. GOD gives his people peace.

PSALM 29:11 THE MESSAGE

A child has been born for us. We have been given a Son who will be our ruler. His names will be Wonderful Advisor and Mighty God, Eternal Father and Prince of Peace.

ISAIAH 9:6 CEV

73

Peace—
When I Need a Quiet Mind

You will keep in perfect peace all who trust in you, whose thoughts are fixed on you! Trust in the Lord always, for the Lord God is the eternal Rock.

ISAIAH 26:3-4

He was pierced for our transgressions, he was crushed for our iniquities; the punishment that brought us peace was upon him, and by his wounds we are healed.

ISAIAH 53:5 NIV

Don't worry over anything whatever; whenever you pray tell God every detail of your needs in thankful prayer, and the peace of God, which surpasses human understanding, will keep constant guard over your hearts and minds as they rest in Christ Jesus.

PHILIPPIANS 4:6-7 PHILLIPS

Persecution—
When I Need the Courage to Face It

The Lord is with me like a mighty warrior;
so my persecutors will stumble and not prevail.
They will fail and be thoroughly disgraced;
their dishonor will never be forgotten.

JEREMIAH 20:11 NIV

"God blesses those who are persecuted
because they live for God, for the Kingdom
of Heaven is theirs. God blesses you when
you are mocked and persecuted and lied
about because you are my followers. Be
happy about it! Be very glad! For a great
reward awaits you in heaven. And remember,
the ancient prophets were persecuted, too."

MATTHEW 5:10-12

If people persecute you because you are a
Christian, don't curse them; pray that God
will bless them.

ROMANS 12:14

Persecution—
When I Need the Courage to Face It

This priceless treasure we hold, so to speak, in common earthenware—to show that the splendid power of it belongs to God and not to us. We are hard-pressed on all sides, but we are never frustrated; we are puzzled, but never in despair. We are persecuted, but are never deserted: we may be knocked down but we are never knocked out! Every day we experience something of the death of Jesus, so that we may also show the power of the life of Jesus in these bodies of ours. Yes, we who are living are always being exposed to death for Jesus' sake, so that the life of Jesus may be plainly seen in our mortal lives. We are always facing physical death, so that you may know spiritual life. Our faith is like that mentioned in the scripture: I believed and therefore did I speak.

2 CORINTHIANS 4:7-13 PHILLIPS

Persecution—
When I Need the Courage to Face It

"I tell you to love your enemies and pray for anyone who mistreats you. Then you will be acting like your Father in heaven. He makes the sun rise on both good and bad people. And he sends rain for the ones who do right and for the ones who do wrong."

MATTHEW 5:44-45 CEV

In times of trouble, you will protect me. You will hide me in your tent and keep me safe on top of a mighty rock.

PSALM 27:5 CEV

Dear brothers and sisters, whenever trouble comes your way, let it be an opportunity for joy. For when your faith is tested, your endurance has a chance to grow. So let it grow, for when your endurance is fully developed, you will be strong in character and ready for anything.

JAMES 1:2-4

Pressure—
When I Feel I'm about to Be Crushed

"Come to me, all of you who are weary
and over-burdened, and I will give you rest!
Put on my yoke and learn from me. For I am
gentle and humble in heart and you will find
rest for your souls. For my yoke is easy and
my burden is light."

MATTHEW 11:28-30 PHILLIPS

My friends, I want you to know what a
hard time we had in Asia. Our sufferings
were so horrible and so unbearable that
death seemed certain. In fact, we felt sure
that we were going to die. But this made us
stop trusting in ourselves and start trusting
God, who raises the dead to life. God saved
us from the threat of death, and we are sure
that he will do it again and again.

2 CORINTHIANS 1:8-10 CEV

GOD's a safe-house for the battered, a
sanctuary during bad times.

PSALM 9:9 THE MESSAGE

Pressure—
When I Feel I'm about to Be Crushed

The Lord is my shepherd; I have everything I need. He lets me rest in green meadows; he leads me beside peaceful streams. He renews my strength. He guides me along right paths, bringing honor to his name.

PSALM 23:1-3

Even though others succumb all around, drop like flies right and left, no harm will even graze you.

PSALM 91:7 THE MESSAGE

Whoever listens to me will live in safety and be at ease, without fear of harm.

PROVERBS 1:33 NIV

Pressure—
When I Feel I'm about to Be Crushed

"I am leaving you with a gift—peace of mind and heart. And the peace I give isn't like the peace the world gives. So don't be troubled or afraid."

JOHN 14:27

Because you belong to Christ Jesus, God will bless you with peace that no one can completely understand. And this peace will control the way you think and feel.

PHILIPPIANS 4:7 CEV

For God has not given us a spirit of cowardice, but a spirit of power and love and a sound mind.

2 TIMOTHY 1:7 PHILLIPS

Cast all your anxiety on him because he cares for you.

1 PETER 5:7 NIV

Rejection—
When Friends Turn Their Back on Me

See how very much our heavenly Father loves us, for he allows us to be called his children, and we really are! But the people who belong to this world don't know God, so they don't understand that we are his children.

1 JOHN 3:1

Friends come and friends go, but a true friend sticks by you like family.

PROVERBS 18:24 THE MESSAGE

For the Lord will not reject his people; he will never forsake his inheritance.

PSALM 94:14 NIV

Rejection—
When Friends Turn Their Back on Me

"When the poor and needy search for water and there is none, and their tongues are parched from thirst, then I, the Lord, will answer them. I, the God of Israel, will never forsake them."

ISAIAH 41:17

He was hated and rejected; his life was filled with sorrow and terrible suffering. No one wanted to look at him. We despised him and said, "He is a nobody!" He suffered and endured great pain for us, but we thought his suffering was punishment from God.

ISAIAH 53:3-4 CEV

The Lord your God is a merciful God; he will not abandon or destroy you or forget the covenant with your forefathers, which he confirmed to them by oath.

DEUTERONOMY 4:31 NIV

Rejection—
When Friends Turn Their Back on Me

"Be strong and courageous! Do not be afraid of them! The Lord your God will go ahead of you. He will neither fail you nor forsake you."

DEUTERONOMY 31:6

Everyone who honors your name can trust you, because you are faithful to all who depend on you.

PSALM 9:10 CEV

Though my father and mother forsake me, the Lord will receive me.

PSALM 27:10 NIV

The Lord answered, "Could a mother forget a child who nurses at her breast? Could she fail to love an infant who came from her own body? Even if a mother could forget, I will never forget you. A picture of your city is drawn on my hand. You are always on my thoughts!"

ISAIAH 49:15-16 CEV

Restoration—
When the Enemy Has Stolen from Me

Restore to me again the joy of your
salvation, and make me willing to obey you.

PSALM 51:12

And after you have borne these sufferings
a very little while, the God of all grace, who
has called you to share his eternal splendour
through Christ, will himself make you whole
and secure and strong. All power is his for
ever and ever, amen!

1 PETER 5:10-11 PHILLIPS

Our God, make us strong again! Smile on
us and save us.

PSALM 80:3 CEV

Restoration—
When the Enemy Has Stolen from Me

Restore us to yourself, O Lord, that we may return; renew our days as of old.

LAMENTATIONS 5:21 NIV

In his justice he will punish those who persecute you. And God will provide rest for you who are being persecuted and also for us when the Lord Jesus appears from heaven.

2 THESSALONIANS 1:6-7

For the land of Israel lies empty and broken after your attacks, but the Lord will restore its honor and power again.

NAHUM 2:2

Restoration—
When the Enemy Has Stolen from Me

He restores my soul. He guides me in
paths of righteousness for his name's sake.

PSALM 23:3 NIV

You kept me from the hands of my
enemies, and you set me free.

PSALM 31:8 CEV

"A thief is only there to steal and kill and
destroy. I came so they can have real and
eternal life, more and better life than they
ever dreamed of."

JOHN 10:10 THE MESSAGE

Salvation—
When I Need to Be Sure

Sin *pays* its servants: the wage is death.
But God *gives* to those who serve him: his
free gift is eternal life through Jesus Christ
our Lord.

ROMANS 6:23 PHILLIPS

For if you confess with your mouth that
Jesus is Lord and believe in your heart that
God raised him from the dead, you will be
saved. For it is by believing in your heart
that you are made right with God, and it is
by confessing with your mouth that you
are saved.

ROMANS 10:9-10

"This is how much God loved the world:
He gave his Son, his one and only Son. And
this is why: so that no one need be
destroyed; by believing in him, anyone can
have a whole and lasting life."

JOHN 3:16 THE MESSAGE

Salvation—
When I Need to Be Sure

But if we freely admit that we have sinned, we find him reliable and just—he forgives our sins and makes us thoroughly clean from all that is evil.

1 JOHN 1:9 PHILLIPS

God our Savior showed us how good and kind he is. He saved us because of his mercy, and not because of any good things that we have done. God washed us by the power of the Holy Spirit. He gave us new birth and a fresh beginning. God sent Jesus Christ our Savior to give us his Spirit. Jesus treated us much better than we deserve. He made us acceptable to God and gave us the hope of eternal life.

TITUS 3:4-7 CEV

For it is by grace you have been saved, through faith—and this not from yourselves, it is the gift of God.

EPHESIANS 2:8 NIV

Salvation—
When I Need to Be Sure

But even though we were dead in our sins God, who is rich in mercy, because of the great love he had for us, gave us life together with Christ—it is, remember, by grace that you are saved—and has lifted us to take our place with him in Christ Jesus in the Heavens.

EPHESIANS 2:4-5 PHILLIPS

All who call out to the Lord will be saved.

ROMANS 10:13 CEV

Now that we are set right with God by means of this sacrificial death, the consummate blood sacrifice, there is no longer a question of being at odds with God in any way. If, when we were at our worst, we were put on friendly terms with God by the sacrificial death of his Son, now that we're at our best, just think of how our lives will expand and deepen by means of his resurrection life!

ROMANS 5:9-10 THE MESSAGE

Separation—
When God Seems Far Away

"Everything and everyone that the Father has given me will come to me, and I won't turn any of them away."

JOHN 6:37 CEV

My sheep recognise my voice and I know who they are. They follow me and I give them eternal life. They will never die and no one can snatch them out of my hand. My Father, who has given them to me, is greater than all. And no one can snatch anything out of the Father's hand. I and the Father are One."

JOHN 10:27-30 PHILLIPS

The eternal God is your refuge, and his everlasting arms are under you. He thrusts out the enemy before you; it is he who cries, 'Destroy them!'

DEUTERONOMY 33:27

Separation—
When God Seems Far Away

"The Lord himself goes before you and will be with you; he will never leave you nor forsake you. Do not be afraid; do not be discouraged."

DEUTERONOMY 31:8 NIV

I am sure that nothing can separate us from God's love—not life or death, not angels or spirits, not the present or the future, and not powers above or powers below. Nothing in all creation can separate us from God's love for us in Christ Jesus our Lord!

ROMANS 8:38-39 CEV

You're the closest of all to me, GOD, and all your judgments are true. I've known all along from the evidence of your words that you meant them to last forever.

PSALM 119:150-151 THE MESSAGE

Separation—
When God Seems Far Away

The Lord is close to all who call on him,
yes, to all who call on him sincerely.

PSALM 145:18

From the bottom of the pit, I prayed to
you, Lord. I begged you to listen. "Help!" I
shouted. "Save me!" You answered my
prayer and came when I was in need. You
told me, "Don't worry!" You rescued me and
saved my life.

LAMENTATIONS 3:55-58 CEV

Because you are my help, I sing in the
shadow of your wings. My soul clings to you;
your right hand upholds me.

PSALM 63:7-8 NIV

Strength—
When I Feel Weak

The Lord is my strength and my song; he has become my salvation. He is my God, and I will praise him, my father's God, and I will exalt him.

EXODUS 15:2 NIV

You alone are God! Only you are a mighty rock. You are my strong fortress, and you set me free.

2 SAMUEL 22:32-33 CEV

The gods of other nations are merely idols, but the Lord made the heavens! Honor and majesty surround him; strength and beauty are in his dwelling.

1 CHRONICLES 16:26-27

Strength—
When I Feel Weak

I love you, GOD—you make me strong.
GOD is bedrock under my feet, the castle in
which I live, my rescuing knight.

PSALM 18:1 THE MESSAGE

You give me strength and guide me right.
You make my feet run as fast as those of a deer,
and you help me stand on the mountains.

PSALM 18:32-33 CEV

The Lord is my strength and my shield;
my heart trusts in him, and I am helped. My
heart leaps for joy and I will give thanks to
him in song.

PSALM 28:7 NIV

Strength—
When I Feel Weak

My health may fail, and my spirit may grow weak, but God remains the strength of my heart; he is mine forever.

PSALM 73:26

You bless all who depend on you for their strength and all who deeply desire to visit your temple. When they reach Dry Valley, springs start flowing, and the autumn rain fills it with pools of water. Your people grow stronger, and you, the God of gods, will be seen in Zion.

PSALM 84:5-7 CEV

I am ready for anything through the strength of the One who lives within me.

PHILIPPIANS 4:13 PHILLIPS

I Want to Grow in God—

When You Desire
Spiritual Maturity

Discipline—
When I Want to Learn Obedience

"But consider the joy of those corrected by God! Do not despise the chastening of the Almighty when you sin. For though he wounds, he also bandages. He strikes, but his hands also heal."

JOB 5:17-18

My child, don't turn away or become bitter when the Lord corrects you. The Lord corrects everyone he loves, just as parents correct their favorite child.

PROVERBS 3:11-12 CEV

If you love learning, you love the discipline that goes with it—how shortsighted to refuse correction!

PROVERBS 12:1 THE MESSAGE

Discipline—
When I Want to Learn Obedience

He who ignores discipline despises himself, but whoever heeds correction gains understanding.

PROVERBS 15:32 NIV

Bear what you have to bear as "chastening"—as God's dealing with you as sons. No true son ever grows up uncorrected by his father. For if you had no experience of the correction which all sons have to bear you might well doubt the legitimacy of your sonship. After all, when we were children we had fathers who corrected us, and we respected them for it. Can we not much more readily submit to the discipline of the Father of men's souls, and learn how to live?

HEBREWS 12:7-9 PHILLIPS

Behave like obedient children. Don't let your lives be controlled by your desires, as they used to be. Always live as God's holy people should, because God is the one who chose you, and he is holy. That's why the Scriptures say, "I am the holy God, and you must be holy too."

1 PETER 1:14-16 CEV

Discipline—
When I Want to Learn Obedience

No discipline is enjoyable while it is happening—it is painful! But afterward there will be a quiet harvest of right living for those who are trained in this way.

HEBREWS 12:11

You *belong* to the power which you choose to obey, whether you choose sin, whose reward is death, or God, obedience to whom means the reward of righteousness. Thank God that you, who were at one time the servants of sin, honestly responded to the impact of Christ's teaching when you came under its influence. Then, released from the service of sin, you entered the service of righteousness.

ROMANS 6:16-18 PHILLIPS

Our Lord, you bless everyone that you instruct and teach by using your law. You give them rest from their troubles, until a pit can be dug for the wicked.

PSALM 94:12-13 CEV

Faith—
When I Want to Be Stronger

Then Jesus told them, "I assure you, if you have faith and don't doubt, you can do things like this and much more. You can even say to this mountain, 'May God lift you up and throw you into the sea,' and it will happen. If you believe, you will receive whatever you ask for in prayer."

MATTHEW 21:21-22

God promised Abraham a lot of descendants. And when it all seemed hopeless, Abraham still had faith in God and became the ancestor of many nations. Abraham's faith never became weak, not even when he was nearly a hundred years old. He knew that he was almost dead and that his wife Sarah could not have children. But Abraham never doubted or questioned God's promise. His faith made him strong, and he gave all the credit to God. Abraham was certain that God could do what he had promised.

ROMANS 4:18-21 CEV

Faith—
When I Want to Be Stronger

Consequently, faith comes from hearing the message, and the message is heard through the word of Christ.

ROMANS 10:17 NIV

It's what we trust in but don't yet see that keeps us going.

2 CORINTHIANS 5:7 THE MESSAGE

Above all be sure you take faith as your shield, for it can quench every burning missile the enemy hurls at you.

EPHESIANS 6:16 PHILLIPS

What is faith? It is the confident assurance that what we hope for is going to happen. It is the evidence of things we cannot yet see. God gave his approval to people in days of old because of their faith. By faith we understand that the entire universe was formed at God's command, that what we now see did not come from anything that can be seen.

HEBREWS 11:1-3

Faith—
When I Want to Be Stronger

"I tell you for certain that if you have faith in me, you will do the same things that I am doing. You will do even greater things, now that I am going back to the Father."

JOHN 14:12 CEV

For I am not ashamed of the gospel. I see it as the very power of God working for the salvation of everyone who believes it, for the Jew first but also for the Greek. I see in it God's plan for making men right in his sight, a process begun and continued by their faith. For, as the scripture says: The righteous shall live by faith.

ROMANS 1:16-17 PHILLIPS

When people work, their wages are not a gift. Workers earn what they receive. But people are declared righteous because of their faith, not because of their work.

ROMANS 4:4-5

Hunger—
When I Want More of God

O Lord, by your hand save me from such men, from men of this world whose reward is in this life. You still the hunger of those you cherish; their sons have plenty, and they store up wealth for their children. And I—in righteousness I will see your face; when I awake, I will be satisfied with seeing your likeness.

PSALM 17:14-15 NIV

"You're blessed when you've worked up a good appetite for God. He's food and drink in the best meal you'll ever eat."

MATTHEW 5:6 THE MESSAGE

"God blesses you who are hungry now, for you will be satisfied. God blesses you who weep now, for the time will come when you will laugh with joy."

LUKE 6:21

Hunger—
When I Want More of God

Let them give thanks to the Lord for his unfailing love and his wonderful deeds for men, for he satisfies the thirsty and fills the hungry with good things.

PSALM 107:8-9 NIV

God—you're my God! I can't get enough of you! I've worked up such hunger and thirst for God, traveling across dry and weary deserts. So here I am in the place of worship, eyes open, drinking in your strength and glory. In your generous love I am really living at last! My lips brim praises like fountains.

PSALM 63:1-3 THE MESSAGE

God is the one who began this good work in you, and I am certain that he won't stop before it is complete on the day that Christ Jesus returns.

PHILIPPIANS 1:6 CEV

Hunger—
When I Want More of God

Let us go right into the presence of God, with true hearts fully trusting him. For our evil consciences have been sprinkled with Christ's blood to make us clean, and our bodies have been washed with pure water.

HEBREWS 10:22

Ask me, and I will tell you things that you don't know and can't find out.

JEREMIAH 33:3 CEV

The poor will see and be glad—you who seek God, may your hearts live!

PSALM 69:32 NIV

Patience—
When I Need to Wait

A man's wisdom gives him patience; it is to his glory to overlook an offense.

PROVERBS 19:11 NIV

Something completed is better than something just begun; patience is better than too much pride.

ECCLESIASTES 7:8 CEV

But when the Holy Spirit controls our lives, he will produce this kind of fruit in us: love, joy, peace, patience, kindness, goodness, faithfulness, gentleness, and self-control. Here there is no conflict with the law.

GALATIANS 5:22-23

Patience—
When I Need to Wait

And we pray this in order that you may live a life worthy of the Lord and may please him in every way: bearing fruit in every good work, growing in the knowledge of God, being strengthened with all power according to his glorious might so that you may have great endurance and patience, and joyfully giving thanks to the Father, who has qualified you to share in the inheritance of the saints in the kingdom of light.

COLOSSIANS 1:10-12 NIV

Since God chose you to be the holy people whom he loves, you must clothe yourselves with tenderhearted mercy, kindness, humility, gentleness, and patience.

COLOSSIANS 3:12

It's smart to be patient, but it's stupid to lose your temper.

PROVERBS 14:29 CEV

Patience—
When I Need to Wait

Better a patient man than a warrior, a man who controls his temper than one who takes a city.

PROVERBS 16:32 NIV

But be patient, my brothers, as you wait for the Lord to come. Look at the farmer quietly awaiting the precious harvest of his land. See how he has to possess his soul in patience till the early and late rains have fallen. So must you be patient, resting your hearts on the ultimate certainty. The Lord's coming is very near.

JAMES 5:7-8 PHILLIPS

Quiet down before GOD, be prayerful before him. Don't bother with those who climb the ladder, who elbow their way to the top.

PSALM 37:7 THE MESSAGE

Praise—
When I Want to Go Deeper

The Lord is my strength, the reason for my song, because he has saved me. I praise and honor the Lord—he is my God and the God of my ancestors.

EXODUS 15:2 CEV

I will proclaim the name of the Lord; how glorious is our God! He is the Rock; his work is perfect. Everything he does is just and fair. He is a faithful God who does no wrong; how just and upright he is!

DEUTERONOMY 32:3-4

Sing to him, sing praise to him; tell of all his wonderful acts. Glory in his holy name; let the hearts of those who seek the Lord rejoice.

1 CHRONICLES 16:9-10 NIV

Praise—
When I Want to Go Deeper

As they began to sing and praise, the Lord set ambushes against the men of Ammon and Moab and Mount Seir who were invading Judah, and they were defeated.

2 CHRONICLES 20:22 NIV

I'm thanking God, who makes things right. I'm singing the fame of heaven-high GOD.

PSALM 7:17 THE MESSAGE

I will thank you, Lord, with all my heart; I will tell of all the marvelous things you have done. I will be filled with joy because of you. I will sing praises to your name, O Most High.

PSALM 9:1-2

Shout Hallelujah, you God-worshipers; give glory, you sons of Jacob; adore him, you daughters of Israel. He has never let you down, never looked the other way when you were being kicked around. He has never wandered off to do his own thing; he has been right there, listening.

PSALM 22:22-23 THE MESSAGE

Praise—
When I Want to Go Deeper

Thank God, the God and Father of our Lord Jesus Christ, that in his great mercy we have been born again into a life full of hope, through Christ's rising again from the dead!

1 PETER 1:3 PHILLIPS

How we praise God, the Father of our Lord Jesus Christ, who has blessed us with every spiritual blessing in the heavenly realms because we belong to Christ.

EPHESIANS 1:3

Accept one another, then, just as Christ accepted you, in order to bring praise to God.

ROMANS 15:7 NIV

Purity—
When I Want a Clean Heart

He who has clean hands and a pure heart, who does not lift up his soul to an idol or swear by what is false. He will receive blessing from the Lord and vindication from God his Savior.

PSALM 24:4-5 NIV

Create pure thoughts in me and make me faithful again. Don't chase me away from you or take your Holy Spirit away from me. Make me as happy as you did when you saved me; make me want to obey!

PSALM 51:10-12 CEV

How can a young person live a clean life? By carefully reading the map of your Word. I'm single-minded in pursuit of you; don't let me miss the road signs you've posted. I've banked your promises in the vault of my heart so I won't sin myself bankrupt.

PSALM 119:9-11 THE MESSAGE

Purity—
When I Want a Clean Heart

I pray that your love for each other will overflow more and more, and that you will keep on growing in your knowledge and understanding. For I want you to understand what really matters, so that you may live pure and blameless lives until Christ returns. May you always be filled with the fruit of salvation—those good things that are produced in your life by Jesus Christ—for this will bring much glory and praise to God.

PHILIPPIANS 1:9-11

"Don't you see that whatever goes *into* the mouth passes into the stomach and then out of the body altogether? But the things that come *out* of a man's mouth come from his heart and mind, and it is they that really make a man unclean. For it is from a man's mind that evil thoughts arise—murder, adultery, lust, theft, perjury and slander. These are the things which make a man unclean, not eating without washing his hands properly!"

MATTHEW 15:17-20 PHILLIPS

Purity—
When I Want a Clean Heart

Do all you have to do without grumbling or arguing, so that you may be blameless and harmless, faultless children of God, living in a warped and diseased age, and shining like lights in a dark world.

PHILIPPIANS 2:14 PHILLIPS

It was not with goats' or calves' blood but with his own blood that he entered once and for all into the holy place, having won for us men eternal reconciliation with God. For if the blood of bulls and goats and the ashes of a burnt heifer were, when sprinkled on the unholy, sufficient to make the body pure, then how much more will the blood of Christ himself, who in the eternal spirit offered himself to God as the perfect sacrifice, purify our conscience from the deeds of death, that we may serve the living God!

HEBREWS 9:12-14 PHILLIPS

Run from temptations that capture young people. Always do the right thing. Be faithful, loving, and easy to get along with. Worship with people whose hearts are pure.

2 TIMOTHY 2:22 CEV

Success—
When I Want to Know God's Perspective

Respect and serve the Lord! Your reward will be wealth, a long life, and honor.

PROVERBS 22:4 CEV

And it is a good thing to receive wealth from God and the good health to enjoy it. To enjoy your work and accept your lot in life— that is indeed a gift from God.

ECCLESIASTES 5:19

With me are riches and honor, enduring wealth and prosperity. My fruit is better than fine gold; what I yield surpasses choice silver.

PROVERBS 8:18-19 NIV

Success—
When I Want to Know God's Perspective

The homes of the upright—how blessed!
Their houses brim with wealth and a
generosity that never runs dry.

PSALM 112:3 THE MESSAGE

My prayer for you, my very dear friend, is
that you may be as healthy and prosperous in
every way as you are in soul.

3 JOHN 2 PHILLIPS

All you who fear GOD, how blessed you
are! How happily you walk on his smooth
straight road! You worked hard and deserve
all you've got coming. Enjoy the blessing!
Revel in the goodness!

PSALM 128:1-2 THE MESSAGE

Success—
When I Want to Know God's Perspective

Do not let this Book of the Law depart from your mouth; meditate on it day and night, so that you may be careful to do everything written in it. Then you will be prosperous and successful.

JOSHUA 1:8 NIV

They are like trees planted along the riverbank, bearing fruit each season without fail. Their leaves never wither, and in all they do, they prosper.

PSALM 1:3

I [wisdom] can make you rich and famous, important and successful. What you receive from me is more valuable than even the finest gold or the purest silver. I always do what is right, and I give great riches to everyone who loves me.

PROVERBS 8:18-21 CEV

Wisdom—
When I Want to Know God's Ways

You desire honesty from the heart, so you can teach me to be wise in my inmost being.

PSALM 51:6

The wisdom that comes from above is first pure, then peace-loving, gentle, approachable, full of merciful thoughts and kindly actions, straight-forward with no hint of hypocrisy. And the peacemakers go on quietly sowing for a harvest of righteousness.

JAMES 3:17-18 PHILLIPS

Teach us to number our days aright, that we may gain a heart of wisdom.

PSALM 90:12 NIV

Wisdom—
When I Want to Know God's Ways

Reverence for the Lord is the foundation of true wisdom. The rewards of wisdom come to all who obey him. Praise his name forever!

PSALM 111:10

Pay close attention, friend, to what your father tells you; never forget what you learned at your mother's knee. Wear their counsel like flowers in your hair, like rings on your fingers.

PROVERBS 1:8-9 THE MESSAGE

And if, in the process, any of you does not know how to meet any particular problem he has only to ask God—who gives generously to all men without making them feel guilty—and he may be quite sure that the necessary wisdom will be given him.

JAMES 1:5 PHILLIPS

Wisdom—
When I Want to Know God's Ways

All wisdom comes from the Lord, and so do common sense and understanding.

PROVERBS 2:6 CEV

Getting wisdom is the most important thing you can do! And whatever else you do, get good judgment. If you prize wisdom, she will exalt you. Embrace her and she will honor you. She will place a lovely wreath on your head; she will present you with a beautiful crown.

PROVERBS 4:7-9

The fear of the Lord teaches a man wisdom and humility comes before honor.

PROVERBS 15:33 NIV

Worry—
When I Want to Learn to Rest in Him

Pile your troubles on GOD's shoulders—
he'll carry your load, he'll help you out. He'll
never let good people topple into ruin.

PSALM 55:22 THE MESSAGE

"That is why I say to you, don't worry
about living—wondering what you are going
to eat or drink, or what you are going to
wear. Surely life is more important than food,
and the body more important than the
clothes you wear. Look at the birds in the
sky. They never sow nor reap nor store away
in barns, and yet your Heavenly Father feeds
them. Aren't you much more valuable to him
than they are? Can any of you, however
much he worries, make himself even a few
inches taller?"

MATTHEW 6:25-27 PHILLIPS

Do not be anxious about anything, but in
everything, by prayer and petition, with
thanksgiving, present your requests to God.
And the peace of God, which transcends all
understanding, will guard your hearts and
your minds in Christ Jesus.

PHILIPPIANS 4:6-7 NIV

Worry—
When I Want to Learn to Rest in Him

Then Jesus said, "Come to me, all of you who are weary and carry heavy burdens, and I will give you rest. Take my yoke upon you. Let me teach you, because I am humble and gentle, and you will find rest for your souls."

MATTHEW 11:28-29

God, the one and only—I'll wait as long as he says. Everything I need comes from him, so why not?

PSALM 62:1 THE MESSAGE

Live under the protection of God Most High and stay in the shadow of God All-Powerful. Then you will say to the Lord, "You are my fortress, my place of safety; you are my God, and I trust you."

PSALM 91:1-2 CEV

Worry—
When I Want to Learn to Rest in Him

Trust GOD from the bottom of your heart; don't try to figure out everything on your own. Listen for GOD's voice in everything you do, everywhere you go; he's the one who will keep you on track.

PROVERBS 3:5-6 THE MESSAGE

Commit everything you do to the Lord. Trust him, and he will help you.

PSALM 37:5

Don't fret or worry. Instead of worrying, pray. Let petitions and praises shape your worries into prayers, letting God know your concerns. Before you know it, a sense of God's wholeness, everything coming together for good, will come and settle you down. It's wonderful what happens when Christ displaces worry at the center of your life.

1 PETER 5:7 THE MESSAGE

I Want to Get Beyond Myself—

When You Want to Be More
"Others Minded"

Church—
When I Want to Know
How to Be a Part of the Body

Together you are the body of Christ. Each one of you is part of his body. First, God chose some people to be apostles and prophets and teachers for the church. But he also chose some to work miracles or heal the sick or help others or be leaders or speak different kinds of languages.

1 CORINTHIANS 12:27-28 CEV

His "gifts unto men" were varied. Some he made his messengers, some prophets, some preachers of the gospel; to some he gave the power to guide and teach his people. His gifts were made that Christians might be properly equipped for their service, that the whole body might be built up until the time comes when, in the unity of common faith and common knowledge of the Son of God, we arrive at real maturity—that measure of development which is meant by "the fulness of Christ".

EPHESIANS 4:11-13 PHILLIPS

Church—
When I Want to Know
How to Be a Part of the Body

Show respect for everyone. Love your
Christian brothers and sisters. Fear God.
Show respect for the king.

1 PETER 2:17

How wonderful, how beautiful, when
brothers and sisters get along!

PSALM 133:1 THE MESSAGE

Just as our bodies have many parts and
each part has a special function, so it is with
Christ's body. We are all parts of his one
body, and each of us has different work to
do. And since we are all one body in Christ,
we belong to each other, and each of us
needs all the others.

ROMANS 12:4-5

There is one body and one Spirit—just as
you were called to one hope when you were
called—one Lord, one faith, one baptism;
one God and Father of all, who is over all
and through all and in all.

EPHESIANS 4:4-6 NIV

Church—
When I Want to Know
How to Be a Part of the Body

"And the king will reply, 'I assure you that whatever you did for the humblest of my brothers you did for me.'"

MATTHEW 25:40 PHILLIPS

Let's see how inventive we can be in encouraging love and helping out, not avoiding worshiping together as some do but spurring each other on, especially as we see the big Day approaching.

HEBREWS 10:24-25 THE MESSAGE

Let the peace of Christ rule in your hearts, since as members of one body you were called to peace. And be thankful.

COLOSSIANS 3:15 NIV

Friendship—
When I Want to Be a Godly Friend

A friend loves at all times, and a brother is
born for adversity.

PROVERBS 17:17 NIV

There are "friends" who destroy each
other, but a real friend sticks closer than
a brother.

PROVERBS 18:24

The king is the friend of all who are
sincere and speak with kindness.

PROVERBS 22:11 CEV

Friendship—
When I Want to Be a Godly Friend

Wounds from a friend are better than many kisses from an enemy.

PROVERBS 27:6

You are better off to have a friend than to be all alone, because then you will get more enjoyment out of what you earn. If you fall, your friend can help you up. But if you fall without having a friend nearby, you are really in trouble.

ECCLESIASTES 4:9-10 CEV

Troublemakers start fights; gossips break up friendships.

PROVERBS 16:28 THE MESSAGE

Friendship—
When I Want to Be a Godly Friend

Perfume and incense bring joy to the heart, and the pleasantness of one's friend springs from his earnest counsel.

PROVERBS 27:9 NIV

Overlook an offense and bond a friendship; fasten on to a slight and—goodbye, friend!

PROVERBS 17:9 THE MESSAGE

As iron sharpens iron, a friend sharpens a friend.

PROVERBS 27:17

A righteous man is cautious in friendship, but the way of the wicked leads them astray.

PROVERBS 12:26 NIV

Giving—
What Does God's Word
Say about Generosity?

Good will comes to him who is generous
and lends freely, who conducts his affairs
with justice.

PSALM 112:5 NIV

"So, when you do good to other people,
don't hire a trumpeter to go in front of you—
like those play-actors in the synagogues and
streets who make sure that men admire
them. Believe me, they have had all the
reward they are going to get! No, when you
give to charity, don't even let your left hand
know what your right hand is doing, so that
your giving may be secret. Your Father who
knows all secrets will reward you."

MATTHEW 6:2-4 PHILLIPS

The world of the generous gets larger and
larger; the world of the stingy gets smaller
and smaller. The one who blesses others is
abundantly blessed; those who help others
are helped.

PROVERBS 11:24-25 THE MESSAGE

Giving—
What Does God's Word Say about Generosity?

Blessed are those who are generous, because they feed the poor.

PROVERBS 22:9

He who gives the seed to the sower and bread to eat, will give you the seed of generosity to sow and will make it grow into a harvest of good deeds done. The more you are enriched the more scope will there be for generous giving, and your gifts, administered through us, will mean that many will thank God.

2 CORINTHIANS 9:10-11 PHILLIPS

You do everything better than anyone else. You have stronger faith. You speak better and know more. You are eager to give, and you love us better. Now you must give more generously than anyone else.

2 CORINTHIANS 8:7 CEV

Giving—
What Does God's Word Say about Generosity?

"Give and men will give to you—yes, good measure, pressed down, shaken together and running over will they pour into your lap. For whatever measure you use with other people, they will use in their dealings with you."

LUKE 6:38 PHILLIPS

Remember this—a farmer who plants only a few seeds will get a small crop. But the one who plants generously will get a generous crop. You must each make up your own mind as to how much you should give. Don't give reluctantly or in response to pressure. For God loves the person who gives cheerfully. And God will generously provide all you need. Then you will always have everything you need and plenty left over to share with others. As the Scriptures say, "Godly people give generously to the poor. Their good deeds will never be forgotten."

2 CORINTHIANS 9:6-9

Gratitude—
When I Want to Quit Thinking "Poor Me"

Just as you received Christ Jesus the Lord, so go on living in him—in simple faith. Yes, be rooted in him and founded upon him, continually strengthened by the faith as you were taught it, and your lives will overflow with joy and thankfulness.

COLOSSIANS 2:6-7 PHILLIPS

Whatever you do or say, let it be as a representative of the Lord Jesus, all the while giving thanks through him to God the Father.

COLOSSIANS 3:17

Thank God for letting our Lord Jesus Christ give us the victory!

1 CORINTHIANS 15:57 CEV

Gratitude—
When I Want to Quit Thinking "Poor Me"

Be cheerful no matter what; pray all the time; thank God no matter what happens. This is the way God wants you who belong to Christ Jesus to live.

1 THESSALONIANS 5:18 THE MESSAGE

Give thanks to the Lord, for he is good; his love endures forever.

PSALM 107:1 NIV

Since then we have been given a kingdom that is "unshakable," let us serve God with thankfulness in the ways which please him, but always with reverence and holy fear. For it is perfectly true that our God is a burning fire.

HEBREWS 12:28-29 PHILLIPS

Gratitude—
When I Want to Quit Thinking "Poor Me"

Don't worry about anything, but pray about everything. With thankful hearts offer up your prayers and requests to God.

PHILIPPIANS 4:6 CEV

Thank God for his marvelous love, for his miracle mercy to the children he loves; offer thanksgiving sacrifices, tell the world what he's done—sing it out!

PSALM 107:21 THE MESSAGE

Let us come before him with thanksgiving. Let us sing him psalms of praise. For the Lord is a great God, the great King above all gods.

PSALM 95:2-3

Loving Others—
When I Need a Push
in the Right Direction

I pray that your love for each other will overflow more and more, and that you will keep on growing in your knowledge and understanding.

PHILIPPIANS 1:9

May the Lord give you the same increasing and overflowing love for each other and towards all men as we have towards you. May he establish you, holy and blameless in heart and soul, before God, the Father of us all, when our Lord Jesus comes with all who belong to him.

1 THESSALONIANS 3:12-13 PHILLIPS

Next, as regards brotherly love, you don't need any written instructions. God himself is teaching you to love each other, and you are already extending your love to all the Macedonians. Yet we urge you to have more and more of this love, and to make it your ambition to have, in a sense, no ambition!

1 THESSALONIANS 4:9-10 PHILLIPS

Loving Others—
When I Need a Push
in the Right Direction

I pray that the Lord will guide you to be as loving as God and as patient as Christ.

2 THESSALONIANS 3:5 CEV

This is real love. It is not that we loved God, but that he loved us and sent his Son as a sacrifice to take away our sins. Dear friends, since God loved us that much, we surely ought to love each other. No one has ever seen God. But if we love each other, God lives in us, and his love has been brought to full expression through us.

1 JOHN 4:10-12

Hope does not disappoint us, because God has poured out his love into our hearts by the Holy Spirit, whom he has given us.

ROMANS 5:5 NIV

Loving Others—
When I Need a Push
in the Right Direction

"Now I am giving you a new command—
love one another. Just as I have loved you, so
you must love one another. This is how all
men will know that you are my disciples,
because you have such love for one another."

JOHN 13:34-35 PHILLIPS

Everything in the world is about to be
wrapped up, so take nothing for granted.
Stay wide-awake in prayer. Most of all, love
each other as if your life depended on it.
Love makes up for practically anything.

1 PETER 4:8 THE MESSAGE

If anyone says, "I am living in the light,"
but hates a Christian brother or sister, that
person is still living in darkness. Anyone
who loves other Christians is living in the
light and does not cause anyone to stumble.

1 JOHN 2:9-10

Poor—
When I Need to Know How to Respond

"But if there are any poor people in your towns when you arrive in the land the Lord your God is giving you, do not be hard-hearted or tightfisted toward them. Instead, be generous and lend them whatever they need."

DEUTERONOMY 15:7-8

He raises the poor from the dust and lifts the needy from the ash heap; he seats them with princes and has them inherit a throne of honor. "For the foundations of the earth are the Lord's; upon them he has set the world."

1 SAMUEL 2:8 NIV

Every bone in my body will shout: "No one is like the Lord!" You protect the helpless from those in power; you save the poor and needy from those who hurt them.

PSALM 35:10 CEV

Poor—
When I Need to Know How to Respond

If you obey the royal Law, expressed by
the scripture, "Thou shalt love thy neighbour
as thyself", all is well.

JAMES 2:8 PHILLIPS

Then he turned to his host. "When you
put on a luncheon or a dinner," he said,
"don't invite your friends, brothers, relatives,
and rich neighbors. For they will repay you
by inviting you back. Instead, invite the
poor, the crippled, the lame, and the blind.
Then at the resurrection of the godly, God
will reward you for inviting those who could
not repay you."

LUKE 14:12-14

Do not oppress the widow or the
fatherless, the alien or the poor. In your
hearts do not think evil of each other.

ZECHARIAH 7:10 NIV

Poor—
When I Need to Know How to Respond

More cedar in your palace doesn't make you a better king than your father Josiah. He always did right—he gave justice to the poor and was honest. That's what it means to truly know me. So he lived a comfortable life and always had enough to eat and drink.

JEREMIAH 22:15-16 CEV

"And the king will reply, 'I assure you that whatever you did for the humblest of my brothers you did for me.'"

MATTHEW 25:40 PHILLIPS

Pure and lasting religion in the sight of God our Father means that we must care for orphans and widows in their troubles, and refuse to let the world corrupt us.

JAMES 1:27

What If I Stumble?—

What If You Fall into Sin?

Anger—
When I Need to Cool Off

Stop your anger! Turn from your rage! Do not envy others—it only leads to harm.

PSALM 37:8

It's smart to be patient, but it's stupid to lose your temper.

PROVERBS 14:29 CEV

Better a patient man than a warrior, a man who controls his temper than one who takes a city.

PROVERBS 16:32 NIV

Anger—
When I Need to Cool Off

Smart people know how to hold their tongue; their grandeur is to forgive and forget.

PROVERBS 19:11 THE MESSAGE

Don't be quick-tempered, for anger is the friend of fools.

ECCLESIASTES 7:9

If our minds are ruled by our desires, we will die. But if our minds are ruled by the Spirit, we will have life and peace.

ROMANS 8:6 CEV

Anger—
When I Need to Cool Off

Let there be no more bitter resentment or anger, no more shouting or slander, and let there be no bad feeling of any kind among you. Be kind to each other; be compassionate. Be as ready to forgive others as God for Christ's sake has forgiven you.

EPHESIANS 4:31-32 PHILLIPS

Do nothing out of selfish ambition or vain conceit, but in humility consider others better than yourselves.

PHILIPPIANS 2:3 NIV

Knowing this, then, dear brothers, let every man be quick to listen but slow to use his tongue, and slow to lose his temper. For man's temper is never the means of achieving God's true goodness.

JAMES 1:19-20 PHILLIPS

Condemnation—
When I Just Can't
Remember I'm Forgiven

My dear children, I write this to you so
that you will not sin. But if anybody does sin,
we have one who speaks to the Father in our
defense—Jesus Christ, the Righteous One.
He is the atoning sacrifice for our sins, and
not only for ours but also for the sins of the
whole world.

1 JOHN 2:1-2 NIV

Christ died once for our sins. An innocent
person died for those who are guilty. Christ
did this to bring you to God, when his body
was put to death and his spirit was made alive.

1 PETER 3:18 CEV

But when the kindness and love of God
our saviour dawned upon us, he saved us in
his mercy— not by virtue of any moral
achievement of ours, but by the cleansing
power of a new birth and the renewal of the
Holy Spirit, which he poured upon us
through Jesus Christ our Saviour. The result
is that we are acquitted by his grace, and can
look forward in hope to inheriting life eternal.

TITUS 3:4-8 PHILLIPS

Condemnation—
When I Just Can't Remember I'm Forgiven

We see, then, that as one act of sin exposed the whole race of men to God's judgment and condemnation, so one act of perfect righteousness presents all men freely acquitted in the sight of God. One man's disobedience placed all men under the threat of condemnation, but one man's obedience has the power to present all men righteous before God.

ROMANS 5:18-19 PHILLIPS

"Oh, what joy for those whose disobedience is forgiven, whose sins are put out of sight. Yes, what joy for those whose sin is no longer counted against them by the Lord."

ROMANS 4:7-8

He used his servant body to carry our sins to the Cross so we could be rid of sin, free to live the right way. His wounds became your healing.

1 PETER 2:24 THE MESSAGE

Condemnation—
When I Just Can't Remember I'm Forgiven

For God caused Christ, who himself knew nothing of sin, actually to *be* sin for our sakes, so that in Christ we might be made good with the goodness of God.

2 CORINTHIANS 5:21 PHILLIPS

As high as heaven is over the earth, so strong is his love to those who fear him. And as far as sunrise is from sunset, he has separated us from our sins.

PSALM 103:12 THE MESSAGE

So now there is no condemnation for those who belong to Christ Jesus. For the power of the life-giving Spirit has freed you through Christ Jesus from the power of sin that leads to death.

ROMANS 8:1-2

Forgiveness—
When I Want to Be Restored to God

Create in me a clean heart, O God. Renew a right spirit within me. Do not banish me from your presence, and don't take your Holy Spirit from me. Restore to me again the joy of your salvation, and make me willing to obey you.

PSALM 51:10-12

But if we freely admit that we have sinned, we find him utterly reliable and just—he forgives our sins and makes us thoroughly clean from all that is evil.

1 JOHN 1:9 PHILLIPS

Christ sacrificed his life's blood to set us free, which means that our sins are now forgiven. Christ did this because God was so kind to us. God has great wisdom and understanding, and by what Christ has done, God has shown us his own mysterious ways.

EPHESIANS 1:7-9 CEV

Forgiveness—
When I Want to Be Restored to God

He has not punished us for all our sins,
nor does he deal with us as we deserve. For
his unfailing love toward those who fear him
is as great as the height of the heavens above
the earth.

PSALM 103:10-11

He has forgiven you all your sins: he has
utterly wiped out the written evidence of
broken commandments which always hung
over our heads, and has completely annulled
it by nailing it to the cross.

COLOSSIANS 2:13 PHILLIPS

Then I let it all out; I said, "I'll make a
clean breast of my failures to God." Suddenly
the pressure was gone—my guilt dissolved,
my sin disappeared.

PSALM 32:5-6 THE MESSAGE

Forgiveness—
When I Want to Be Restored to God

"This is the covenant I will make with them after that time, says the Lord. I will put my laws in their hearts, and I will write them on their minds." Then he adds: "Their sins and lawless acts I will remember no more." And where these have been forgiven, there is no longer any sacrifice for sin.

HEBREWS 10:16-18 NIV

I write this letter to you all, as my dear children, because your sins are forgiven for his name's sake.

1 JOHN 2:12 PHILLIPS

We all arrive at your doorstep sooner or later, loaded with guilt, our sins too much for us—but you get rid of them once and for all.

PSALM 65:2-3 THE MESSAGE

Grudges—
When I Need to Forgive and Let It Go

"'Do not seek revenge or bear a grudge against one of your people, but love your neighbor as yourself. I am the Lord.'"

LEVITICUS 19:18 NIV

Let it be your ambition to live at peace with all men and to achieve holiness "without which no man shall see the Lord." Be careful that none of you fails to respond to the grace of God, for if he does there can spring up in him a bitter spirit which can poison the lives of many others.

HEBREWS 12:14-15 PHILLIPS

Love is patient and kind. Love is not jealous or boastful or proud or rude. Love does not demand its own way. Love is not irritable, and it keeps no record of when it has been wronged.

1 CORINTHIANS 13:4-5

Grudges—
When I Need to Forgive and Let It Go

It's wise to be patient and show what you are like by forgiving others.

PROVERBS 19:11 CEV

"Blessed are the merciful, for they will be shown mercy."

MATTHEW 5:7 NIV

"For if you forgive other people their failures, your Heavenly Father will also forgive you. But if you will not forgive other people, neither will your Father forgive you your failures."

MATTHEW 6:14-15 PHILLIPS

"Whenever you stand up to pray, you must forgive what others have done to you. Then your Father in heaven will forgive your sins."

MARK 11:25 CEV

Grudges—
When I Need to Forgive and Let It Go

"You must be merciful, as your Father is merciful. Don't judge other people and you will not be judged yourselves. Don't condemn and you will not be condemned. Forgive others and people will forgive you."

LUKE 6:36-37 PHILLIPS

"Be alert. If you see your friend going wrong, correct him. If he responds, forgive him. Even if it's personal against you and repeated seven times through the day, and seven times he says, 'I'm sorry, I won't do it again,' forgive him."

LUKE 17:3-4 THE MESSAGE

Dear friends, don't try to get even. Let God take revenge. In the Scriptures the Lord says, "I am the one to take revenge and pay them back."

ROMANS 12:19 CEV

Lust—
When I Want to Have a Pure Heart

My son, keep your father's commands and do not forsake your mother's teaching. Bind them upon your heart forever; fasten them around your neck. When you walk, they will guide you; when you sleep, they will watch over you; when you awake, they will speak to you. For these commands are a lamp, this teaching is a light, and the corrections of discipline are the way to life.

PROVERBS 6:20-23 NIV

May the words of my mouth and the thoughts of my heart be pleasing to you, O Lord, my rock and my redeemer.

PSALM 19:14

Create pure thoughts in me and make me faithful again.

PSALM 51:10 CEV

Lust—
When I Want to Have a Pure Heart

Be concerned with the heavenly things, not with the passing things of earth. For, as far as this world is concerned, you are already dead, and your true life is a hidden one in God, through Christ. One day, Christ, who is your life, will show himself openly, and you will all share in that magnificent revelation. Consider yourselves dead to worldly contacts: have nothing to do with sexual immorality, dirty-mindedness, uncontrolled passion, evil desire, and the lust for other people's goods, which amounts to idolatry.

COLOSSIANS 3:2-5 PHILLIPS

God wants you to be holy, so don't be immoral in matters of sex. Respect and honor your wife. Don't be a slave of your desires or live like people who don't know God.

1 THESSALONIANS 4:3-5 CEV

Lust—
When I Want to Have a Pure Heart

Since Christ suffered physical pain you must arm yourselves with the same inner conviction that he had. To be free from sin means bodily suffering, and the man who accepts this will spend the rest of his time here on earth, not in being led by human desires, but in doing the will of God.

1 PETER 4:1-2 PHILLIPS

Don't love the world's ways. Don't love the world's goods. Love of the world squeezes out love for the Father. Practically everything that goes on in the world—wanting your own way, wanting everything for yourself, wanting to appear important—has nothing to do with the Father. It just isolates you from him. The world and all its wanting, wanting, wanting is on the way out—but whoever does what God wants is set for eternity.

1 JOHN 2:15-17 THE MESSAGE

Lust—
When I Want to Have a Pure Heart

How can a young person stay pure? By obeying your word and following its rules. I have tried my best to find you—don't let me wander from your commands. I have hidden your word in my heart, that I might not sin against you.

PSALM 119:9-11

If this is so, then the Lord knows how to rescue godly men from trials and to hold the unrighteous for the day of judgement, while continuing their punishment.

2 PETER 2:9 NIV

Lying—
When I Want to Walk in Integrity

Truthful lips endure forever, but a lying tongue lasts only a moment.

PROVERBS 12:19 NIV

God can't stomach liars; he loves the company of those who keep their word.

PROVERBS 12:22 THE MESSAGE

A lying tongue hates its victims, and flattery causes ruin.

PROVERBS 26:28

Lying—
When I Want to Walk in Integrity

Giving an honest answer is a sign of true friendship.

PROVERBS 24:26 CEV

The king is pleased with righteous lips; he loves those who speak honestly.

PROVERBS 16:13

Righteousness guards the man of integrity, but wickedness overthrows the sinner.

PROVERBS 13:6 NIV

Train me, GOD, to walk straight; then I'll follow your true path.

PSALM 86:11 THE MESSAGE

Lying—
When I Want to Walk in Integrity

The integrity of the honest keeps them on track; the deviousness of crooks brings them to ruin.

PROVERBS 11:3 THE MESSAGE

In my integrity you uphold me and set me in your presence forever.

PSALM 41:12 NIV

Fling off the dirty clothes of the old way of living, which were rotted through and through with lust's illusions, and, with yourselves mentally and spiritually re-made, to put on the clean fresh clothes of the new life which was made by God's design for righteousness and the holiness which is no illusion. Finish, then, with lying and let each man tell his neighbour the truth, for we are all parts of the same body.

EPHESIANS 4:22-25 PHILLIPS

Mercy—
When I Need It Most

Let us therefore approach the throne of grace with fullest confidence, that we may receive mercy for our failures and grace to help in the hour of need.

HEBREWS 4:16 PHILLIPS

GOD is all mercy and grace—not quick to anger, is rich in love. God is good to one and all; everything he does is suffused with grace.

PSALM 145:8-9 THE MESSAGE

Who is a God like you, who pardons sin and forgives the transgression of the remnant of his inheritance? You do not stay angry forever but delight to show mercy.

MICAH 7:18 NIV

Mercy—
When I Need It Most

O Lord, you are so good, so ready to forgive, so full of unfailing love for all who ask your aid.

PSALM 86:5

You have answered my prayer and my plea for mercy. My enemies will be ashamed and terrified, as they quickly run away in complete disgrace.

PSALM 6:9-10 CEV

Remember, O Lord, your great mercy and love, for they are from old. Remember not the sins of my youth and my rebellious ways; according to your love remember me, for you are good, O Lord.

PSALM 25:6-7 NIV

I love GOD because he listened to me, listened as I begged for mercy.

PSALM 116:1-2 THE MESSAGE

Mercy—
When I Need It Most

For the Mighty One has done great things for me—holy is his name. His mercy extends to those who fear him, from generation to generation.

LUKE 1:49-50 NIV

But even though we were dead in our sins God, who is rich in mercy, because of the great love he had for us, gave us life together with Christ—it is, remember, by grace that you are saved—and has lifted us to take our place with him in Christ Jesus in the Heavens.

EPHESIANS 2:4-5 PHILLIPS

God our Savior showed us how good and kind he is. He saved us because of his mercy, and not because of any good things that we have done. God washed us by the power of the Holy Spirit. He gave us new birth and a fresh beginning.

TITUS 3:4-5 CEV

Shame—
When I Feel I Can't Face God

I asked the Lord for help, and he saved me
from all my fears. Keep your eyes on the
Lord! You will shine like the sun and never
blush with shame.

PSALM 34:4-5 CEV

May my heart be blameless toward your
decrees, that I may not be put to shame.

PSALM 119:80 NIV

The Lord will save the people of Israel
with eternal salvation. They will never again
be humiliated and disgraced throughout
everlasting ages.

ISAIAH 45:17

There is a passage to this effect in
scripture, and it runs like this: Behold, I lay
in Zion a chief corner stone, elect, precious:
and he that believeth on him shall not be put
to shame.

1 PETER 2:6 PHILLIPS

Shame—
When I Feel I Can't Face God

My head is high, GOD, held high; I'm
looking to you, GOD; no hangdog skulking
for me. I've thrown in my lot with you; you
won't embarrass me, will you? Or let my
enemies get the best of me?

PSALM 25:1-3 THE MESSAGE

For it is believing *in the heart* that makes a
man righteous before God, and it is stating
his belief by his own *lips* that confirms his
salvation. And the scripture says: "Whoever
believes in him shall not be disappointed."

ROMANS 10:10-11 PHILLIPS

Whenever we are in need, we should
come bravely before the throne of our
merciful God. There we will be treated with
undeserved kindness, and we will find help.

HEBREWS 4:16 CEV

Shame—
When I Feel I Can't Face God

Don't be afraid or ashamed and don't be
discouraged. You won't be disappointed. Forget
how sinful you were when you were young;
stop feeling ashamed for being left a widow.

ISAIAH 54:4 CEV

Now, what do we conclude? That the
gentiles who never seriously pursued
righteousness, have attained righteousness,
righteousness-by-faith. But Israel, earnestly
following the Law of righteousness, failed to
reach their goal. And why? Because their
minds were fixed on what they achieved
instead of on what they believed. They
tripped over that very stone the scripture
mentions: Behold, I lay in Zion a stone of
stumbling and a rock of offence: And he that
believeth on him shall not be put to shame.

ROMANS 9:30-33 PHILLIPS

If you belong to Christ Jesus, you won't
be punished.

ROMANS 8:1 CEV

Temptation—
When I'm Hanging from the Edge

Put on the full armor of God so that you can take your stand against the devil's schemes.

EPHESIANS 6:11 NIV

Be on your guard and stay awake. Your enemy, the devil, is like a roaring lion, sneaking around to find someone to attack. But you must resist the devil and stay strong in your faith.

1 PETER 5:8 CEV

You may be absolutely certain that the Lord knows how to rescue good men surrounded by temptation, and how to reserve his punishment for the wicked until their day comes.

2 PETER 2:9 PHILLIPS

Temptation—
When I'm Hanging from the Edge

"Keep alert and pray. Otherwise temptation will overpower you. For though the spirit is willing enough, the body is weak."

MARK 14:38

No temptation has come your way that is too hard for flesh and blood to bear. But God can be trusted not to allow you to suffer any temptation beyond your powers of endurance. He will see to it that every temptation has its way out, so that it will be possible for you to bear it.

1 CORINTHIANS 10:13 PHILLIPS

Now that Jesus has suffered and was tempted, he can help anyone else who is tempted.

HEBREWS 2:18 CEV

Temptation—
When I'm Hanging from the Edge

You, dear children, are from God and have overcome them, because the one who is in you is greater than the one who is in the world.

1 JOHN 4:4 NIV

Turn your back on the turbulent desires of youth and give your positive attention to goodness, integrity, love and peace in company with all those who approach the Lord in sincerity.

2 TIMOTHY 2:22 PHILLIPS

Run away from sexual sin! No other sin so clearly affects the body as this one does. For sexual immorality is a sin against your own body.

1 CORINTHIANS 6:18

Who Am I?—

Knowing Who You
Are in Christ

Accepted—
When I Need to Know God's Grace

The curse of the Lord is on the house of the wicked, but his blessing is on the home of the upright. The Lord mocks at mockers, but he shows favor to the humble. The wise inherit honor, but fools are put to shame!

PROVERBS 3:33-35

From the fullness of his grace we have all received one blessing after another. For the law was given through Moses; grace and truth came through Jesus Christ.

JOHN 1:16-17 NIV

We are made right in God's sight when we trust in Jesus Christ to take away our sins. And we all can be saved in this same way, no matter who we are or what we have done. For all have sinned; all fall short of God's glorious standard. Yet now God in his gracious kindness declares us not guilty. He has done this through Christ Jesus, who has freed us by taking away our sins.

ROMANS 3:22-24

Accepted—
When I Need to Know God's Grace

But the gift of God through Christ is a very different matter from the "account rendered" through the sin of Adam. For while as a result of one man's sin death by natural consequence became the common lot of men, it was by the generosity of God, the free giving of the grace of one man Jesus Christ, that the love of God overflowed for the benefit of all men. Nor is the effect of God's gift the same as the effect of that one man's sin. For in the one case one man's sin brought its inevitable judgment, and the result was condemnation. But, in the other, countless men's sins are met with the free gift of grace, and the result is justification before God. For if one man's offence meant that men should be slaves to death all their lives, it is a far greater thing that through another man, Jesus Christ, men by their acceptance of his more than sufficient grace and righteousness, should live their lives victoriously.

ROMANS 5:15-17 PHILLIPS

Accepted—
When I Need to Know God's Grace

But he said to me, "My grace is sufficient for you, for my power is made perfect in weakness." Therefore I will boast all the more gladly about my weaknesses, so that Christ's power may rest on me.

2 CORINTHIANS 12:9 NIV

Christ sacrificed his life's blood to set us free, which means that our sins are now forgiven. Christ did this because God was so kind to us. God has great wisdom and understanding, and by what Christ has done, God has shown us his own mysterious ways.

EPHESIANS 1:7-8 CEV

Accepted—
When I Need to Know God's Grace

Long ago, even before he made the world, God loved us and chose us in Christ to be holy and without fault in his eyes. His unchanging plan has always been to adopt us into his own family by bringing us to himself through Jesus Christ. And this gave him great pleasure. So we praise God for the wonderful kindness he has poured out on us because we belong to his dearly loved Son. He is so rich in kindness that he purchased our freedom through the blood of his Son, and our sins are forgiven. He has showered his kindness on us, along with all wisdom and understanding.

EPHESIANS 1:4-8

When God, our kind and loving Savior God, stepped in, he saved us from all that. It was all his doing; we had nothing to do with it. He gave us a good bath, and we came out of it new people, washed inside and out by the Holy Spirit. Our Savior Jesus poured out new life so generously. God's gift has restored our relationship with him and given us back our lives.

TITUS 3:4-6 THE MESSAGE

Child of God—
When I Need to Know God Is My Father

He came into his own world, and his own people would not accept him. Yet wherever men did accept him he gave them the power to become sons of God. These were the men who truly believed in him, and their birth depended not on natural descent nor on any physical impulse or plan of man, but on God.

JOHN 1:12-13 PHILLIPS

See how very much our heavenly Father loves us, for he allows us to be called his children, and we really are! But the people who belong to this world don't know God, so they don't understand that we are his children. Yes, dear friends, we are already God's children, and we can't even imagine what we will be like when Christ returns. But we do know that when he comes we will be like him, for we will see him as he really is.

1 JOHN 3:1-2

Child of God—
When I Need to Know God Is My Father

For he chose us in him before the creation of the world to be holy and blameless in his sight. In love he predestined us to be adopted as his sons through Jesus Christ, in accordance with his pleasure and will—to the praise of his glorious grace, which he has freely given us in the One he loves.

EPHESIANS 1:4-6 NIV

All who follow the leading of God's Spirit are God's own sons. Nor are you meant to relapse into the old slavish attitude of fear— you have been adopted into the very family circle of God and you can say with a full heart, "Father, my Father." The Spirit himself endorses our inward conviction that we really are the children of God. Think what that means. If we are his children then we are God's heirs, and all that Christ inherits will belong to all of us as well! Yes, if we share in his sufferings we shall certainly share in his glory.

ROMANS 8:14-17 PHILLIPS

Just as parents are kind to their children, the Lord is kind to all who worship him.

PSALM 103:13 CEV

Child of God—
When I Need to Know God Is My Father

For we, remember, are ourselves temples of the living God, as God has said: I will dwell in them and walk in them: and I will be their God, and they shall be my people. Therefore come ye out from among them and be ye separate, saith the Lord, and touch no unclean thing; and I will receive you, and will be to you a Father, and ye shall be to me sons and daughters, saith the Lord Almighty.

2 CORINTHIANS 6:16-18 PHILLIPS

But when the right time came, God sent his Son, born of a woman, subject to the law. God sent him to buy freedom for us who were slaves to the law, so that he could adopt us as his very own children. And because you Gentiles have become his children, God has sent the Spirit of his Son into your hearts, and now you can call God your dear Father. Now you are no longer a slave but God's own child. And since you are his child, everything he has belongs to you.

GALATIANS 4:4-7

Chosen—
When I Need to Know I Belong

For you are a holy people, who belong to the Lord your God. Of all the people on earth, the Lord your God has chosen you to be his own special treasure.

DEUTERONOMY 7:6

So too, at the present time there is a remnant chosen by grace. And if by grace, then it is no longer by works; if it were, grace would no longer be grace.

ROMANS 11:5-6 NIV

In Christ we have been given an inheritance, since we were destined for this, by the One who works out all his purposes according to the design of his own will. So that we, in due time, as the first to put our hope in Christ, may bring praise to his glory! And you too trusted him, when you had heard the message of truth, the gospel of your salvation. And after you gave your confidence to him you were, so to speak, stamped with the promised Holy Spirit as a pledge of our inheritance, until the day when God completes the redemption of what is his own; and that will again be to the praise of his glory.

EPHESIANS 1:11-14 PHILLIPS

Chosen—
When I Need to Know I Belong

But you are not like that, for you are a chosen people. You are a kingdom of priests, God's holy nation, his very own possession. This is so you can show others the goodness of God, for he called you out of the darkness into his wonderful light.

1 PETER 2:9

"If you belonged to the world, the world would love its own. But because you do not belong to the world and I have chosen you out of it, the world will hate you. Do you remember what I said to you, 'The servant is not greater than his master?' If they have persecuted me, they will persecute you as well, but if they have followed my teaching, they will also follow yours."

JOHN 15:19-20 PHILLIPS

That is how it is with you, my friends. You are now part of the body of Christ and are dead to the power of the Law. You are free to belong to Christ, who was raised to life so that we could serve God.

ROMANS 7:4 CEV

Chosen—
When I Need to Know I Belong

In fact God has arranged the parts in the body, every one of them, just as he wanted them to be. If they were all one part, where would the body be? As it is, there are many parts, but one body.

1 CORINTHIANS 12:18-20 NIV

My children, let us not love merely in theory or in words—let us love in sincerity and in practice! This is how we shall know that we are children of the truth and can reassure ourselves in the sight of God, even if our own conscience makes us feel guilty. For God is greater than our conscience, and he knows everything.

1 JOHN 3:18-20 PHILLIPS

See, I have engraved you on the palms of my hands; your walls are ever before me.

ISAIAH 49:16 NIV

Confidence—
When I Need to Know What I'm Made Of

"Be strong and courageous. Do not be afraid or discouraged because of the king of Assyria and the vast army with him, for there is a greater power with us than with him. With him is only the arm of flesh, but with us is the Lord our God to help us and to fight our battles." And the people gained confidence from what Hezekiah the king of Judah said.

2 CHRONICLES 32:7-8 NIV

You keep me going when times are tough— my bedrock, God, since my childhood.

PSALM 71:5 THE MESSAGE

You need not be afraid of disaster or the destruction that comes upon the wicked, for the Lord is your security. He will keep your foot from being caught in a trap.

PROVERBS 3:25-26

Confidence—
When I Need to Know What I'm Made Of

The fruit of righteousness will be peace;
the effect of righteousness will be quietness
and confidence forever.

ISAIAH 32:17 NIV

I bless those who trust me. They will be
like trees growing beside a stream—trees
with roots that reach down to the water, and
with leaves that are always green. They bear
fruit every year and are never worried by a
lack of rain.

JEREMIAH 17:7-8 CEV

We dare to say such things because of the
confidence we have in God through Christ.
Not that we are in any way confident of
doing anything by our own resources—our
ability comes from God who makes us
competent administrators of the new
agreement, concerned not with the letter but
in the Spirit.

2 CORINTHIANS 3:4-5 PHILLIPS

Confidence—
When I Need to Know What I'm Made Of

It is in this same Jesus, because we have faith in him, that we dare, even with confidence, to approach God.

EPHESIANS 3:12 PHILLIPS

So, friends, we can now—without hesitation—walk right up to God, into "the Holy Place." Jesus has cleared the way by the blood of his sacrifice, acting as our priest before God. The "curtain" into God's presence is his body. So let's *do* it—full of belief, confident that we're presentable inside and out. Let's keep a firm grip on the promises that keep us going. He always keeps his word.

HEBREWS 10:19-22 THE MESSAGE

Dear friends, if we feel at ease in the presence of God, we will have the courage to come near him. He will give us whatever we ask, because we obey him and do what pleases him.

1 JOHN 3:21-22 CEV

Recreated—
When I Need to Remember
I'm No Longer the Same

Since you have heard all about him and have learned the truth that is in Jesus, throw off your old evil nature and your former way of life, which is rotten through and through, full of lust and deception. Instead, there must be a spiritual renewal of your thoughts and attitudes. You must display a new nature because you are a new person, created in God's likeness—righteous, holy, and true.

EPHESIANS 4:21-24

If we have, as it were, shared his death, we shall also share in his resurrection. Let us never forget that our old selves died with him on the cross that the tyranny of sin over us might be broken—for a dead man can safely be said to be free from the power of sin. And if we were dead men with Christ we can believe that we shall also be men alive with him.

ROMANS 6:6-7 PHILLIPS

Recreated—
When I Need to Remember
I'm No Longer the Same

I have died, but Christ lives in me. And I
now live by faith in the Son of God, who
loved me and gave his life for me.

GALATIANS 2:20 CEV

Those who belong to Christ Jesus have
crucified the sinful nature with its passions
and desires. Since we live by the Spirit, let us
keep in step with the Spirit.

GALATIANS 5:24-25 NIV

For if a man is in Christ he becomes a new
person altogether—the past is finished and
gone, everything has become fresh and new.

2 CORINTHIANS 5:17 PHILLIPS

You obeyed the truth, and your souls were
made pure. Now you sincerely love each
other. But you must keep on loving with all
your heart. Do this because God has given you
new birth by his message that lives on forever.

1 PETER 1:22-23 CEV

Recreated—
When I Need to Remember I'm No Longer the Same

Don't lie to each other, for you have stripped off your old evil nature and all its wicked deeds. In its place you have clothed yourselves with a brand-new nature that is continually being renewed as you learn more and more about Christ, who created this new nature within you.

COLOSSIANS 3:9-10

I will give you a new heart and put a new spirit in you; I will remove from you your heart of stone and give you a heart of flesh.

EZEKIEL 36:26 NIV

Righteousness—
What Gives Me the Right to Come to God?

He himself bore our sins in his body on the tree, so that we might die to sins and live for righteousness; by his wounds you have been healed.

1 PETER 2:24 NIV

I don't turn my back on God's undeserved kindness. If we can be acceptable to God by obeying the Law, it was useless for Christ to die.

GALATIANS 2:21 CEV

The course that I was set I have finished, and I have kept the faith. The future for me holds the crown of righteousness which the Lord, the true judge, will give to me in that day—and not, of course, only to me but to all those who have loved what they have seen of him.

2 TIMOTHY 4:7-8 PHILLIPS

About dc Talk

Toby McKeehan   **Michael Tait**   **Kevin Max**

Since releasing their album *Jesus Freak,* dc Talk has emerged as a leader in the pursuit of melding rock 'n' roll with provocative questions of faith.

Although various rock predecessors have examined spiritual issues—U2, Van Morrison, and Bob Dylan immediately come to mind—dc Talk has taken the notion to new lengths, both in commercial terms and depth of artistic exploration. Numerous Dove Awards, three Grammy Awards, one multi-platinum album, two platinum albums, two gold albums, and two gold-certified long-form videos attest to the group's ability to bridge the gap between religious and secular audiences.

Toby, Michael, and Kevin first met in the mid-80s while attending college in Virginia. After relocating to Nashville, dc Talk released a series of increasingly ambitious—and successful—albums, beginning with their self-titled 1989 debut; followed by their gold-certified 1990 sophomore album *Nu Thang;* the platinum-certified 1992 opus *Free at Last;* 1995's *Jesus Freak,* a double-platinum watershed that afforded the group more mainstream success than ever before; and 1998's platinum-selling *Supernatural.*

In 2000, while on a hiatus from recording and traveling, the group released *intermission,* a greatest hits recording that also included two brand-new songs. Since then, each member has released multiple solo projects.

Their first book, *Jesus Freaks,* has had a tremendous impact. The stories of true Jesus Freaks have challenged young people to stand up for their Savior. Upcoming *Jesus Freaks* books will encourage those who were touched by *Jesus Freaks* to go deeper in their relationship with the Lord.